ALONE
AGAINST
THE ATLANTIC

THE STORY OF THE OBSERVER SINGLEHANDED TRANSATLANTIC RACE 1960-80

BY FRANK PAGE

GW00319457

© The Observer Limited 1980
Published by The Observer Limited
8, St. Andrew's Hill, London EC4V 5JA
Printed by Impact Litho
(Tolworth) Limited
ISBN No. 0 9507034 1 9

CONTENTS

CHAPTER 1

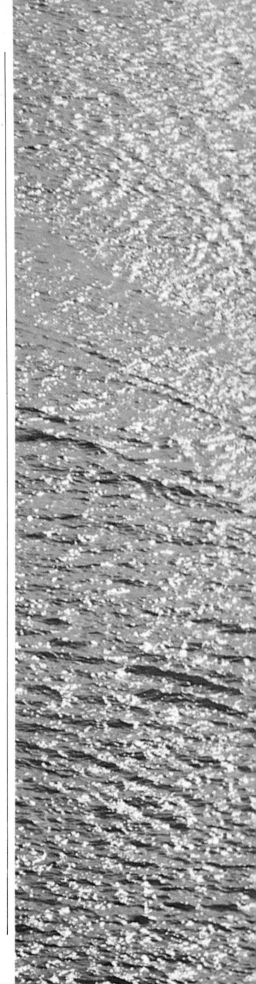

"WHAT AM I DOING HERE?"

A SINGLEHANDED SAILOR once said to me, 'When you go ocean racing you get tired, cold, wet, miserable and sea-sick. When you race across the ocean singlehanded you are all of that – and lonely too.'

To sail across the Atlantic alone in a yacht does seem a particularly refined form of masochism. Yet more and more men, and women, want to do it. When the Royal Western Yacht Club decided to limit the size of the fleet for the 1980 Royal Western/Observer Singlehanded Transatlantic Race to 110 yachts, the list was filled a full year before the race was due to set out from Plymouth. And the 20-year history of the event is a story of constant expansion: bigger and bigger boats, ever-larger fleets, more and more countries entering. Only the limits on size of fleet and overall yacht size set for the 1980 race have curbed this swelling endeavour.

It's not as though the solo skippers eager to pit themselves against the North Atlantic could possibly be unaware of the hazards and terrors of the voyage. There is now a considerable library of books on the race, not to speak of the unwritten legends which are repeated at yacht club bars whenever singlehanders gather. Some of those books contain accounts of storm-tossed voyages which could be expected to make the most ambitious solo yachtsman think again.

The late David Blagden wrote a very honest book about his race in the 1972 Observer Singlehanded (called *'Very Willing Griffin')* and included a transcript of a tape recording he made at the height of a vicious storm and the depths of his own despair. It makes magnetic reading.

'Oh it's been absolute hell and I just don't understand how I could be so stupid (sobbing). (Crash. The boat gets laid flat by a wave). Oh Christ...Oh God I deserve everything I get...and I thought "Well, the other boats, they managed, they got through the Gulf Stream". But of course a big boat can get through the Gulf Stream. I can't even get through a four-foot wave and I knew that when I started. I knew it and I said it and I said it and I said it. 'Oh God, oh Sandy, Sandy...(sobbing)...how could you love somebody so stupid...'

Yet when I spoke to David Blagden at the end of that 1972 race, the

Over the years, the Observer Singlehanded has prompted the development of many fast but sometimes fallible trimarans. A solo skipper who sets out to cross the Atlantic in a craft such as *Three Cheers,* the famous trimaran built for Tom Follett to sail in the 1972 race — must constantly calculate the variables of the speed and safety equation.

Nick Keig, builder and skipper of all the very fast *Three Legs of Mann* trimarans, is forever protesting his own lack of courage. Yet he sailed the *Mark III* boat to a splendid second place in 1980, only nine hours behind the winner.

miseries of mid-Atlantic were forgotten. He boasted how nothing had broken on his tiny 19-footer, how he had not even started a stitch in the sails. He was exultant. It was the song of the man who has come though.

And that seems to be the secret of the hypnotic appeal of this great event: it is a challenge to the strength and stamina and seamanship of any yachtsman; a challenge which has to be met totally alone. Any skipper who completes the course, whether in 18 days or 48, can hold his head high for the rest of his life – it is still no mean feat to have been captain and crew, cook and boathand, navigator and foredeckman on a passage across 3,000 miles of contemptuous ocean into the teeth of the prevailing winds and currents.

The most famous singlehanded sailor of all must be the late Sir Francis Chichester. He won the very first Observer Singlehanded Race in 1960 after helping to get the series started, sailed the course again two years later, crossed yet again in the 1964 race (finishing second to Eric Tabarly) and then went off to prepare for his epic circumnavigation alone. What could have prompted him to set himself ever more difficult targets at an age when most men would have been content to sit back and watch the younger generation flex their muscles?

Fame is a spur, certainly, and so are, for some, financial rewards from books, television appearances and films. But the underlying motive must be to meet that ultimate challenge – to do the whole thing alone; to make one's own mistakes or master-strokes; to be captain of one's fate. After all, there are very few real tests of man's endeavour which can be undertaken entirely alone these days. Mountaineers, explorers, fliers and those most exciting of all adventurers in our time, the space travellers: all are heavily dependent on their fellows. But the solo yachtsman succeeds or fails almost entirely by his own strengths or weaknesses, his own resolution or fallibility, his own ultimate resources.

That is why David Blagden was brave enough to publish the transcript of his recorded monologue. He had been to the brink and come back. That is why Francis Chichester was able to analyse his delight in solo sailing in his book 'Alone Across the Atlantic', written after his victory in the 1960 Observer race. 'Somehow, I never seemed to enjoy so much doing things with other people. I know I don't do a thing nearly as well when with someone. It makes me think I was cut out for solo jobs, and any attempt to diverge from that lot only makes me a half-person.'

But if the singlehanders are tempted by the solo challenge, they also have another common characteristic: they are all courageous. For no matter how well-built the yacht, how strong the rig, how well-prepared the equipment and how experienced the skipper, there is still the insidious element of chance which can bring disaster and danger to the lone voyager. And it takes courage to recognise that possiblity and still want to go. In the North Atlantic, the weather can never be taken for granted. 'Prevailing winds have a habit of not prevailing', said Blondie Hasler, the race's originator. And that could be the least of a skipper's troubles. A freak squall, a sudden bank of fog, a total absence of wind when your boat is in the middle of a shipping lane, even the spine-chilling sight of a looming iceberg: all those hazards lie in wait.

Then there are the natural and man-made dangers. To the layman it might well look as though a singlehander crossing the Atlantic simply sailed out of Plymouth, turned right and kept going until he reached America. Not at all. If he sails the northern route, there are the Scillies to negotiate once he has turned the Lizard. Then he must skirt Cape Race at the tip of Newfoundland, watch out for Sable Island and Cape Sable off Nova Scotia, and navigate with great caution across the shoals and fogs of George's Bank, Cape Cod and Nantucket before finally crossing the finishing line at the Brenton Tower just outside Newport. If he goes south, to the longer route below the Gulf Stream, he must beware first how he navigates past Ushant at the north-west tip of France, avoid getting drawn into the storms and calms of Biscay, then – above all – make sure he skirts the Azores Islands, not sail into them. After that he can start to worry about cutting back north across the Gulf Stream to the final challenges of the Nantucket shoals.

But at least the solo skipper, like the mountaineer, has a wide variety of modern equipment which makes his task easier. The principles of the race, which have remained unaltered throughout its history, include the phrase 'to encourage the development of suitable boats, gear, supplies and techniques for singlehanded ocean crossings under sail'. It's clear that the six Observer Singlehanded races which have been run since those words were first written have certainly done that. They have pushed along the development of self-steering gear (both wind-driven and electric), self-tailing winches, solar panels for electricity generation, furling and roll-away sails, and a host of lesser ideas to ease the labours and perils of handling a yacht alone at sea.

Of those, the greatest aid of all must be self-steering gear. It is true that some competitors in the race have covered huge distances without self-steering; indeed, Eric Tabarly was first to Newport in both 1964 and 1976 having sailed more than half the passage without automatic steering. But for lessor mortals the magic hand at the tiller or wheel is vital. It enables the solo sailor to change sails, to navigate, to repair his gear, to cook his food, to maintain his log and – most important of all – get some rest, while the yacht sails on.

While conditions are right, that is. At the height of a storm, or when the wind fades to a whisper, it is still the skipper's expert hand at the wheel which is the greatest guarantee of safety. So the history of this great event is spiced with stories of singlehanders who have spent long hours in the cockpit pitting their own limited strength and their frail craft against the fury of the wrathful Atlantic. Cold, tired, wet, hungry and lonely, they have often asked the question, 'What am I doing here?'. But not for long. When the storm passes and the sun begins to shine, there's a chance to dry out and prepare a decent meal. Then there's the joy of noting a good day's run towards Newport in the log and the ineffable satisfaction of knowing it was done entirely by your own efforts, on your own decisions, through your own initiative. That's the real magic of sailing singlehanded to America.

Chris Butler has more reasons than most to pit his stamina and seamanship against the Atlantic. He always sails yachts which he has designed and built at his Welsh boatyard. For him, the trip to America is an extended sea trial, and perhaps the opportunity to gain some valuable publicity for his products.

Every Observer Singlehanded Race since 1960 has been won by a yacht sailing a course between the Great Circle and the Rhumb Line. But some boats following the Azores route have made remarkably quick passages, using the more kindly reaching winds which prevail down there to make up for the extra length of the crossing. The crucial point is to avoid the contrary Gulf Stream current which pervades the mid-Atlantic.

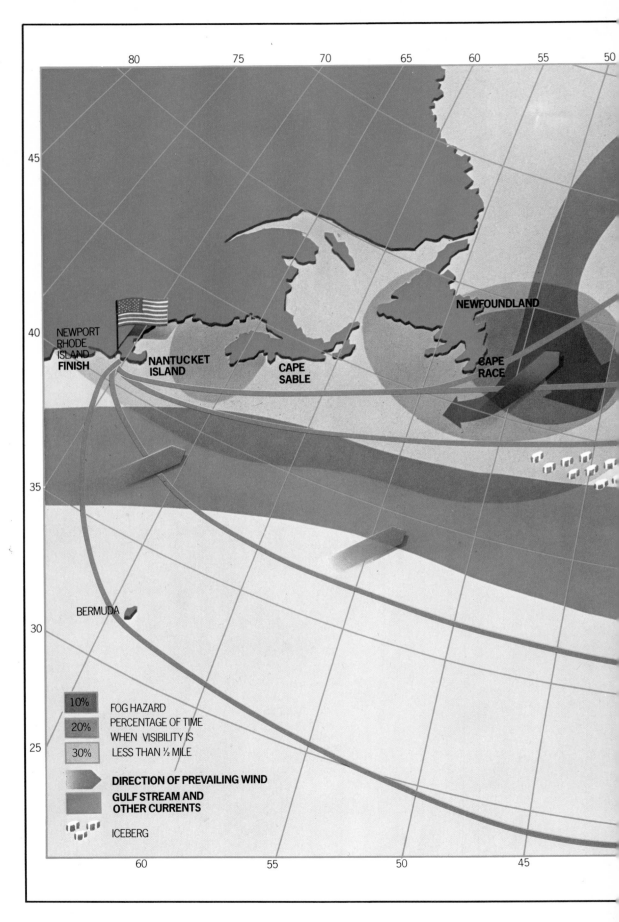

NEWPORT RHODE ISLAND **FINISH**

NANTUCKET ISLAND

CAPE SABLE

NEWFOUNDLAND

CAPE RACE

BERMUDA

10%	FOG HAZARD
20%	PERCENTAGE OF TIME WHEN VISIBILITY IS
30%	LESS THAN ½ MILE

DIRECTION OF PREVAILING WIND

GULF STREAM AND OTHER CURRENTS

ICEBERG

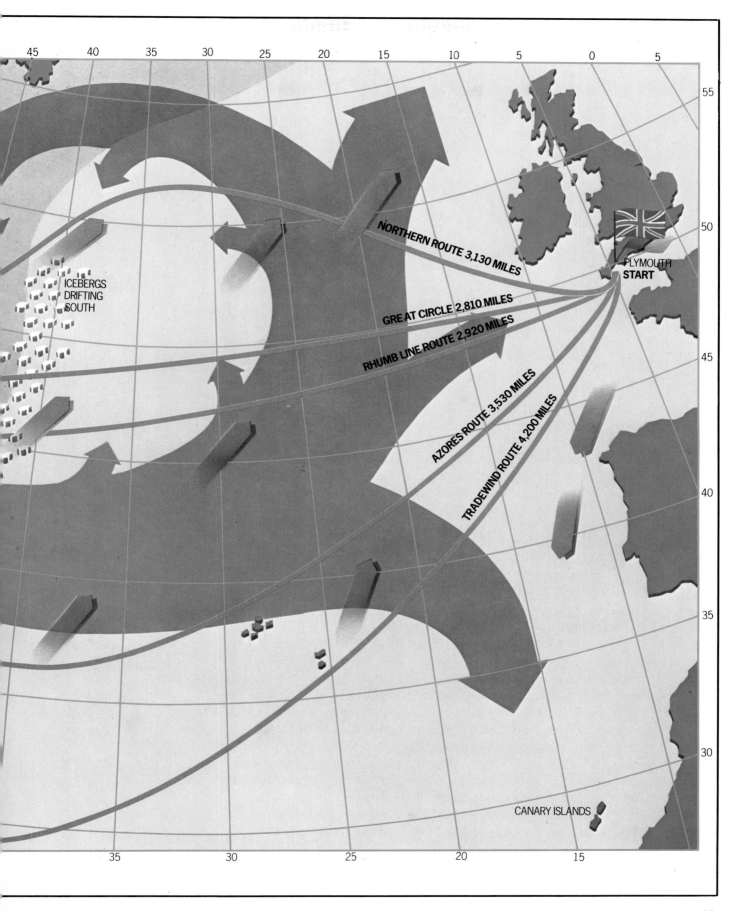

45 40 35 30 25 20 15 10 5 0 5

55

50

ICEBERGS
DRIFTING
SOUTH

NORTHERN ROUTE 3,130 MILES

PLYMOUTH
START

GREAT CIRCLE 2,810 MILES

RHUMB LINE ROUTE 2,920 MILES

45

AZORES ROUTE 3,530 MILES

TRADEWIND ROUTE 4,200 MILES

40

35

30

CANARY ISLANDS

35 30 25 20 15

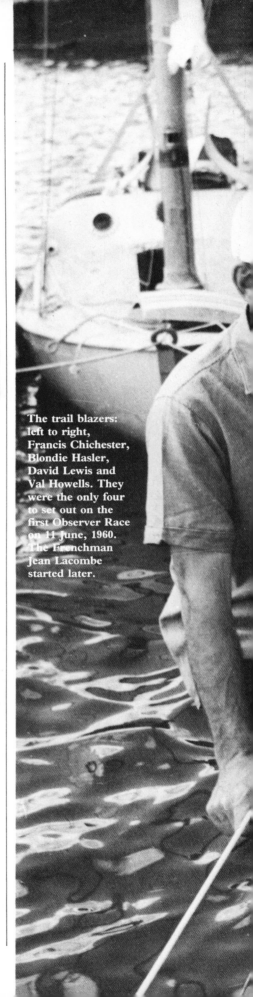

CHAPTER 2

1960—THE PATHFINDERS

THE ROYAL WESTERN YACHT CLUB was persuaded to become the organising club of the first Observer Singlehanded only after several other clubs had turned down the idea. But then, Plymouth's principal yacht club has always been somewhat out of the run of normal yacht clubs. One of the oldest in the country, the Royal Western has always been involved in new events. The very first Fastnet Race, in 1925, was sailed under its burgee; the club ran races for the fabulous 'J' class yachts in the inter-war years; in 1950 it was the finishing point of the Royal Ocean Racing Club's transatlantic race and in 1967 it became the start and finish point of Sir Francis Chichester's famous singlehanded voyage around the world.

The Singlehanded Transatlantic Race was the brainchild of Blondie Hasler, or, to give him his full title, Lt-Col H.G. Hasler, a retired Royal Marines officer. A sailor all his life, Blondie Hasler delighted in experimenting with new forms of rig for sailing boats. His aim was to reduce the miseries of clawing at vast expanses of billowing sails on a bucking foredeck and so conserve the energies of a single- or short-handed skipper. His own yacht *Jester*, a 25-foot Folkboat, had been fitted with an unstayed mast and Chinese lugsail rig, so that she could be trimmed, reefed and unreefed without the skipper needing to go on deck at all – it was all done from a central circular hatch in the domed deck. Hasler believed this was a rig which could take a solo sailor across the Atlantic in safety, without sapping his physical resources. He was prepared to prove the point in a race of singlehanders from Britain to America. It was the sort of challenge to spur another man who liked doing things on his own. Francis Chichester, a map publisher in St James's, London, had made his name by flying huge distances alone in the twenties. By 1960 he had begun using his navigational skill and boundless energy to sail alone. He was so keen to go that he said if no club would organise a race, he would take on Hasler in a boat-to-boat challenge for a half-crown wager.

But the Royal Western did take up the race, despite some misgivings, and The Observer agreed to sponsor the event. So the rules were published and the first entries came in. There were more than 50 enquiries as the

The trail blazers: left to right, Francis Chichester, Blondie Hasler, David Lewis and Val Howells. They were the only four to set out on the first Observer Race on 11 June, 1960. The Frenchman Jean Lacombe started later.

Francis Chichester's 39 foot *Gipsy Moth III* was easily the biggest yacht in the first race. The primitive-looking self-steering gear on her stern was affectionately known as Miranda. Right, the experienced navigator had already developed his taste for the long-peaked caps which became an instant recognition signal.

word about the race spread, with potential entries from the United States, Germany, Denmark and Canada to back up the main interest in Britain and France. But in the end only eight firm entries resulted, and of those just four actually set out for New York on 11 June, 1960, with a fifth to follow later.

It was hardly an imposing fleet. Chichester's 39-foot *Gipsy Moth III* was easily the largest boat; the rest were all 25-footers. Hasler's *Jester* – he called her that because she was 'such a bloody joke' – was matched by a conventionally-rigged Folkboat called *Eira* sailed by the big black-bearded Welshman Val Howells and a Vertue class sloop named *Cardinal Vertue* sailed by Dr David Lewis. The fifth yacht marked the beginning of a continuing tradition – it was a 21-foot sloop called *Cap Horn*, sailed by the Frenchman Jean Lacombe. It started late and finished last, taking longer to reach America than any boat in the race's history – 74 days. But it was the start of the great French fascination with this race. At the 10 a.m. start on that historic day in June, 1960, Blondie Hasler was actually first across the line. Lewis came next, with Howells third and Chichester the last to get into his stride. But the greater waterline length of *Gipsy Moth III* quickly told, and the 58-year-old navigator was soon showing the others the way to the Lizard. Lewis didn't get there that day. His yacht snapped her mast just 3½ hours after the start and he returned to Plymouth for rapid repairs, setting out again the following Monday. He was still ahead of Lacombe, who did not head out of the Sound until the following Thursday.

But then, the 1960 race was a very leisurely affair. Chichester was plugging on gamely along the Great Circle route, while Hasler headed off north to try to find easterly winds on the top side of the Atlantic depressions. Lewis also took the most direct route, but Howells and Lacombe went away south-west in search of warmer seas and more kindly reaching winds.

News of the race for those waiting at home was sparse indeed. Chris Brasher, then Sports Editor of The Observer and a key figure in the newspaper's sponsorship of the event, had little to report in the first two weeks, even though he learned later that there was plenty going on.

Francis Chichester wrote of gale-force winds the second night out, recorded in his log with characteristic verve: 'My word, some whacking big seas hit the hull at times. The noise these seas make is terrific. So much

Below on *Gipsy Moth*. Chichester was a great believer in natural foods and ate a lot of fruit. His wife Sheila added the homely touches.

that I several times started getting out of my berth thinking the yacht had been struck by a steamer or that the mast had gone overboard.'

Then, a fortnight out, *Gipsy Moth* ran into a full storm. 'The din was appalling', wrote the skipper. 'A high-pitched screech dominating everything, spray peppering everywhere and seas hitting periodically with the bonk of a big drum...I put the wind now at 100 m.p.h....I hope those other poor devils have not been caught in this. I am sure it would be much worse in a smaller boat. Personally, I am flogged to the bone.'

Two days later Chichester was about half-way across, with Lewis 375 miles behind him and Hasler away to the north-west, sitting out what he called 'a very boring gale that has been blowing for three days and shows no sign of stopping. If I were cruising I should be comfortably hove-to. As things are, I am driving the poor little thing into a filthy breaking sea with four reefs down.' Howells was by that time near the Azores, with his mind 'boggling at the thought of spending another five weeks in this manner. Have finished all the reading matter – very, very bored.' Lacombe was still off Cape Finisterre, en route to the Azores, so the five yachts had scattered across the ocean in all directions like sparks from a catherine wheel.

A week later it was clear that Chichester was well ahead, with only Hasler close enough to make a race of it. And that is how the pattern developed, until at the end of the fifth week Brasher was predicting a first arrival at New York within a couple of days. It turned out to be wishful thinking; in that first race, as in all those which followed it, the final stages were drawn out and toughened by head winds and calms. Chichester sighted his first land – Block Island – and recorded in his diary, 'I quite understand why people used to, and still do, go into retreat. During a month alone I think at last you become a real person and are concerned with the real value of life.'

Next day, 40 days after setting out from Plymouth, Chichester sailed *Gipsy Moth III* past the Ambrose light at the entrance to New York, which was the finish line for that first race. But not without some misgivings in the final hours. 'Twenty-four miles to go,' he wrote. 'What do you think? Will that black-bearded Viking (Howells) be in already?'.

He need not have worried. The Welsh skipper had been slowed by persistent problems. First a broken battery spilled acid over his food and spare clothes. Then a troublesome leak meant he had to spend hours pumping to keep *Eira* dry. Finally, a knock down in a belt of squalls caused

Chichester urges *Gipsy Moth* along on a broad reach. Yacht design has changed enormously in 20 years and what was then a fast and modern boat now looks strangely old-fashioned, with her raised coach roof, cabin ventilator and hanked-on headsail.

the loss of Howells's chronometer. Without any means of establishing his longitude, he was forced to sail down his latitude to Bermuda, arriving there on 30 July and taking the opportunity of relieving his boredom by staying over until 5 August. That meant he finished fourth, behind Hasler and Lewis, who had finished 8 and 16 days later than Chichester – it was that easy-paced a race.

Hasler was delighted to record that his self-steering had worked so well that he had spent only one hour at the tiller during the whole voyage. Lewis reported a hazardous end to the crossing. He sailed *Cardinal Vertue* along the coast of Nova Scotia in thick fog, then decided to cut inside Martha's Vineyard (a course not allowed in any later race) through Pollock Rip at night and in dense mist, with a vicious tide under his keel. He actually went aground at one point but managed to get off and sail on down to New York, to finish in 56 days, compared with the winner's 40 days and Hasler's time of 48 days.

Those seem very long passages now, in the light of the 1980 race, when no less than 62 yachts made the crossing to Newport, Rhode Island quicker than Chichester's *Gipsy Moth*. But at that time a 40-day crossing was considered astonishingly quick, even if the winner claimed, at his press conference, that he had been aiming at 30 days. 'I hoped to set a time that would be difficult to beat', he said. 'But every time I tried to point *Gipsy Moth* to New York the wind blew dead on the nose. It was like trying to reach a doorway with a man in it aiming a hose at you. It was much tougher than I thought.'

But the main point was proven: a singlehanded transatlantic race was possible, given well-found yachts and adequate self-steering gear. Nobody had been in serious danger; all five yachts had arrived. The race had been a success. Now it was on to 1964 and a bigger and better event.

Top left. Blondie Hasler had just about enough room to live comfortably below in *Jester*. Her Chinese lugsail rig, below left, may not make her very fast, but it means the skipper can shorten sail easily through his hatch without having to claw at acres of flapping sailcloth. Val Howells, below, was called 'The black-bearded Viking' by Chichester.

Dr David Lewis, left, was born in Britain but spent most of his early life in New Zealand. His 25-footer *Cardinal Vertue* was a heavily-built cruising yacht, with a modest sail plan, so his 56 day crossing was not really as slow as it seems by the standards of the 1980 race.

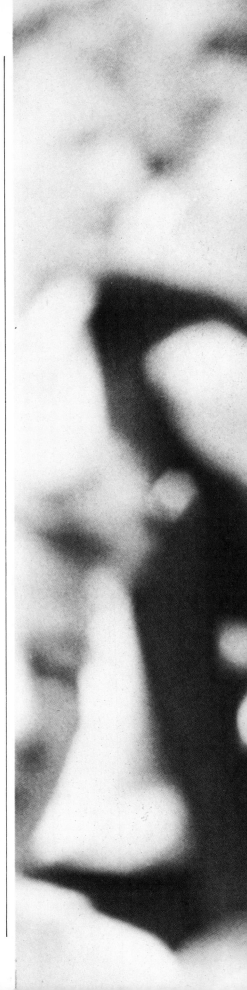

CHAPTER 3

1964–TABARLY'S TRIUMPH

THE FIRST OBSERVER SINGLEHANDED had been a small, friendly, almost parochial affair. The Observer had reported it, of course, but the rest of the world's media hardly stirred when Chichester reached New York. When the others took so much longer to come in, interest quickly waned. The 1964 race could hardly have provided a sharper contrast. It was as different as a world title fight is from a supporting bout at the Hackney Baths.

First, there was a much bigger fleet – 15 starters. Second, the race had become truly an international event; there were two Frenchmen this time, a Dane, an Australian and an American in the list. (In fact, the American, Arthur Piver, never got to the start). And third, the Press was really beginning to take notice. The Guardian signed up Chichester and Lewis to provide daily reports, the Daily Mail made a contract with Mike Ellison, the Daily Express was taking reports from Val Howells and, naturally, The Observer was giving the whole event extensive coverage.

In France, too, there was a thirst for information, not only because Jean Lacombe was competing again, but because the second French entry, from a young Navy lieutenant called Eric Tabarly, was an interesting story in itself. Tabarly was then 32, unknown in his own country, but clearly determined to make a name for himself. He had made an intensive study of the first Observer race and designed a yacht specially for the second with the clear intention of winning. Not for him the satisfaction of merely getting to the other side; the stocky, taciturn Breton intended to be there first.

His yacht was a 44-foot ketch called *Pen Duick II*. It seemed enormous to the others as they gathered in Plymouth before the start. There had been some doubts about whether Chichester could handle the 39-foot *Gipsy Moth* on his own – this was even bigger. But *Pen Duick* was specifically designed for singlehanding. The sail plan was comparatively modest, because the boat was so light – 6½ tons – that she would move quickly in the lightest breeze, and her ketch rig and twin headsails meant there were no huge sails for the solo skipper to wrestle up and down.

Who could beat the determined Frenchman? Chichester was back, of

Eric Tabarly was
unknown before he
won the 1964
Observer
Singlehanded.
Thereafter he was
to become the
great father figure
of the sailing
revolution in
France.

The 1964 fleet sets out from Plymouth Sound. The spectator fleet looks sparse, but it was a great contrast to the unnoticed 1960 start, and a collision with one boat forced Howells back for repairs.

As well as the proud French tricolour, Tabarly's *Pen Duick II* sported a Perspex dome so he could keep a lookout from below without putting on foul weather gear.

course, encouraged by a 33-day crossing – a whole week faster than in the first race – in 1962. Hasler and Jester were also going again, and Val Howells had a 35-footer called *Akka* this time. David Lewis had a 40-foot catamaran with the Maori name *Rehu Moana* – it means 'spray'. Another catamaran was to be sailed by Michael Butterfield, and Derek Kelsall had entered the first trimaran in the Observer Singlehanded's history – a 35-foot ketch-rigged yacht to Arthur Piver's design. There was another name in the list which was to become more famous later – Alec Rose had entered his cruising yacht *Lively Lady.*

So it was a much more impressive fleet which set off from Plymouth on Saturday 23 May, 1964. Three of the 15 boats were more than 40 feet and nine measured between 30 and 40 feet – a huge contrast with the gaggle of small boats which had set out four years earlier.

So was the send-off. In 1960 there were just a few spectator craft. In 1964 Plymouth Sound was thronged with power boats, ocean racers, pleasure boats and dinghies, all packed with well-wishers. The air was buzzing with helicopters and light aircraft carrying photographers to record the swelling scene.

This time the target for those 15 yachts was Newport, Rhode Island. New York had proved a difficult port to sail into four years before and the race committee, under its chairman Lt-Col Jack Odling-Smee, decided it was better to finish up the coast at the traditional centre of sailing on the American eastern seaboard. So as Kelsall's *Folatre* led the fleet away, with Hasler and Chichester close behind, they were aiming for a finish line at the Brenton tower outside Newport, as it has been ever since, leaving Nantucket to starboard.

The light easterly wind at the start that year had helped Kelsall's trimaran to set the pace, but not for long. Tabarly hoisted a big spinnaker and surged past *Gipsy Moth* and *Jester* in pursuit of *Folatre*. As so often in this race, the earliest indications were a clear guide to the form for the whole event.

Unfortunately, the spectator fleet provided the first hazard of the race. Val Howells's *Akka* was rammed by one and he had to return for repairs to his boom and self-steering gear. He was later forced into Ireland for repairs to a mast-head block, too, so his eventual third place was a splendid achievement after double delays. The Welshman also showed this time that he had a very shrewd idea of how the race was going. Chichester, Lewis,

Francis Chichester
explains after the 1964
race some of the
many adventures
of his passage to
second place in just
under 30 days. It
had started, right,
with *Gipsy Moth*
going away under
twin boomed-out
headsails.

Pen Duick II was
the first yacht in
the race's history
to be specially
designed to win —
and win she did.

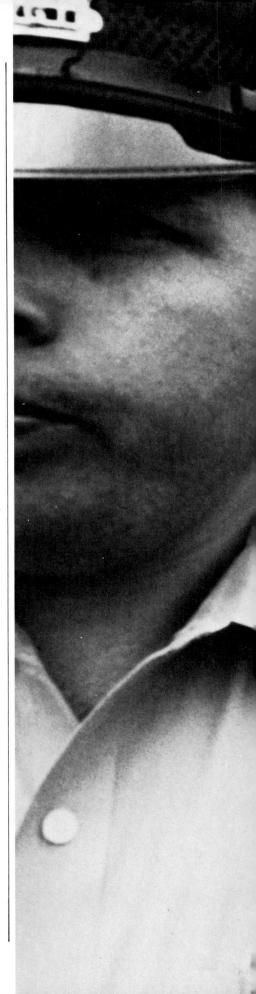

Hero's welcome for Tabarly as he arrives at Newport. President de Gaulle made him a Chevalier of Legion d'Honneur immediately.

Howells and Ellison were constantly reporting their positions. But Tabarly was not, although he had a radio on board – 'I do not like these radio instruments,' he said. That meant the French boat was often missed out of the calculations because her position was never very clear, and for many of those reporting the race it looked as though Chichester was going to repeat his victory of four years earlier, even though Tabarly was sighted in mid-ocean 160 miles ahead of *Gipsy Moth III*.

It was Howells who put the picture into its true perspective. 'Tabarly boyo', he said to the Observer, 'that's the fellow I'd put my wild money on. I make him a day ahead of Francis, and what's more I think Francis knows it. Tabarly has a magnificent boat, he's a fine sailor and he's superbly fit'. Howells estimated that *Pen Duick II* would arrive in America about 21 June. He was two days out.

Chichester, too, was aware of the French threat. He radioed to The Guardian, 'Tabarly is the dark horse in this race and I think I hear him galloping through the night. If my senses tell me right I can make him out about 120 miles to the north.' His senses were remarkably acute.

Meanwhile there were alarums and excursions lower down the fleet. Lewis and Ellison were following on behind Chichester but Kelsall had dropped out of the reckoning. Five days after the start, and when he was possibly just ahead of Tabarly with 550 miles completed, *Folatre* hit something under the water and broke her rudder. 'I hope there's a whale out there with a sore head,' Kelsall said when he limped back into Plymouth for repairs. *Folatre* did set out again, and completed the course to Newport in 35 days – it would have been good enough to give Kelsall fourth place if he had kept going with the rest.

Michael Butterfield's *Misty Miller* and Geoffrey Chaffey's *Ericht 2* were both forced to call into the Azores for repairs, while Robin McCurdy's 41-footer *Tammie Noire* retired because of electrical failures. Hasler's *Jester* and Howells's *Akka* were making fine progress up to the north, where the easterlies were blowing consistently, and Chichester had lost about half a day when *Gipsy Moth* was slowed by a leak in her hull.

Suddenly the picture came into sharp focus. The Canadian Air Force spotted *Pen Duick II* 350 miles from the finish on 15 June. If he could maintain his average of 100 miles a day, Tabarly would be at the finish in little over 27 days on the 19th. He could and he did, sailing into a Newport harbour crammed with the 143 yachts of the Newport-Bermuda race

Lord Mountbatten
presented the
winner's trophy to
Eric Tabarly in the
autumn of 1964 at
a special dinner in
London.

fleet – nobody had thought the first singlehander could possibly have reached the line before the Onion Patch racers went away.

The most astonishing aspect of Tabarly's race was to emerge only after he had acknowledged the cheers and congratulations of the waiting crowds: he had sailed about 2,000 miles of the voyage without self-steering. The gear had broken about one-third of the way across the ocean, and since then he had never slept more than 90 minutes at a time. Indeed, he had been entirely without sleep for the 48 hours before his arrival.

Chichester's comment, when he arrived in second place nearly three days later, was apt: 'He's a cracking good sailor, a hell of a chap and tough as old boots.' President de Gaulle's response was rather more formal. He made Tabarly a Chevalier of the Legion d'Honneur instantly – and the great Tabarly legend had begun. Since then he has become the father figure of yachting in France and the inspiration of so many young, tough, adventurous and talented sailors who were to make their mark on the history of the Observer Singlehanded.

Howells finished third, despite his delays, and Alec Rose was fourth with *Lively Lady*. But the surprise of the early finishers was Hasler's *Jester*. The northern route had certainly paid off, for the little junk-rigged Folkboat arrived in just under 38 days, ten days faster than in the first race and an impressive justification of Hasler's belief that an easily-handled rig enables the solo skipper to push on more consistently because it does not make such heavy demands on his strength and stamina. But in his conclusions on the race, written for The Observer, the race's founder was more concerned to praise the victor: 'Eric Tabarly's win delighted me...The boat was built on a very small budget, and Eric's performance in getting her to the Brenton reef in 27 days, in spite of an unserviceable vane steering gear, must rank very near the summit of singlehanded sailing.' A generous tribute from the expert whose opinion is valued more highly than anybody's in this area of man's endeavour.

CHAPTER 4

1968–THE COMBATIVE CORNISHMAN

THE 1968 OBSERVER SINGLEHANDED RACE was the first of the event's maturity. In the balance of foreign to British competitors, of multihulls to monohulls, of sponsored to non-sponsored boats and of good to bad weather, the 1968 contest proved a classic, and it set the pattern for the races to follow during the next 12 years.

The foreign entry was certainly encouraging, with eight other nations providing 21 entries to battle against the 14 British boats. The first Americans had arrived, and the French challenge had grown to nine yachts. There were three each from Sweden and Germany, plus the first-ever competitor from South Africa – in a yacht called *Voortrekker*, which was to reappear in 1980. More exciting for the media men, as the fleet gathered in Plymouth, was the entry of the first woman singlehander in the race's history. Edith Baumann, a German secretary, had entered a 39-foot trimaran called *Koala III*. But she had been sailing for less than a year and the experts thought she still had a lot to learn. It was hardly surprising to find that Ladbroke's, when they opened a book on the race, put her bottom of the list as a 100/1 outsider. Justly, as it turned out, for the boat sank.

For the multihull enthusiasts, the scene at Plymouth was a delight. No less than 13 of the 35 entries had two or three hulls. More important, the race favourite had arrived with a monster trimaran which looked capable of romping across the ocean almost before the rest had got out of the Channel.

It was Eric Tabarly of course, in his 67-foot aluminium triple-huller *Pen Duick IV*. Like many other sailors, Tabarly had been very impressed by the speed and seaworthiness of Derek Kelsall's trimaran *Toria*, when she won the 1966 Round Britain Race. So he had hastily commissioned the outsize trimaran which was finished only just in time for him to get to Plymouth.

Toria was in the dock too, though now renamed *Gancia Girl*, because she was sponsored by an Italian sparkling wine producer. Her skipper was to be Martin Minter-Kemp. In fact, alcohol-producers set the pace of sponsorship for this race. Leslie Williams sailed a 53-footer called *Spirit of Cutty Sark*, with backing from the whisky company; Bill Howell's

SIR THO

Geoffrey Williams's yacht for the 1968 race was a sleek 56-foot ketch designed by Robert Clark which could slice through the water speedily in a good breeze.

LIPTON

The 1968 start was in almost flat calm. Stephen Pakenham's *Rob Roy* (No 7) and Leslie Williams's *Spirit of Cutty Sark* (No 9) have crept ahead of Guy Piazzini's *Gunther III* (No 34) and *La Delirante* of Lionel Paillard (40).

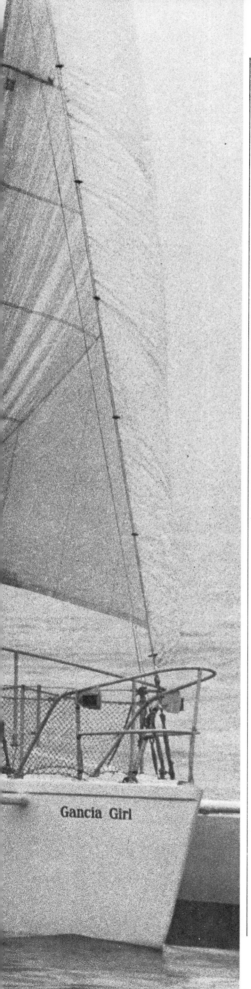

Martin Minter-Kemp sailed *Gancia Girl,* more familiar as the fast trimaran *Toria,* which designer Derek Kelsall and Minter-Kemp had sailed to victory in the Round Britain Race two years earlier.

Gancia Girl

catamaran *Golden Cockerel* was financially assisted by the Courage brewery; and Colin Forbes's trimaran *Startled Faun* had some backing from Watney's. But despite her name, the American entry *Cheers* was not backed by a booze-maker. She was a fascinating schooner-rigged proa designed by a man who was to have a lasting influence on the race – Dick Newick. Sailed by Tom Follett, an experienced American helmsman, *Cheers* looked capable of high speeds in the right conditions, despite her modest length of 40 feet.

Of the rest, the most likely rivals for Tabarly seemed to be a tough young Cornishman called Geoffrey Williams and an equally-determined South African called Bruce Dalling. Williams was sponsored by the Allied Suppliers group (providers of Lipton's tea, among many other things) and he had put their cash into a big 56-foot ketch designed by Robert Clark and called it *Sir Thomas Lipton.* Dalling's yacht *Voortrekker* was also ketch-rigged, but smaller – she measured just over 49 feet. Other likely front runners were *Raph,* a 57-foot French ketch sailed by Alain Gliksman, and *San Giorgio,* a 54-foot catamaran from Italy to be helmed by Alex Carozzo.

Sheer size was of little value when the race started on 1 June. There was so little wind in Plymouth Sound that some of the skippers were reduced to rowing their yachts away from the line. Though the skies were leaden and a steady rain dampened the scene, there were still plenty of spectators at the off. They saw most of the fleet creep away – Edith Baumann decided there was too little wind for her and returned to harbour – with Tabarly, as expected, edging into the lead as the yachts disappeared into the murk.

But Tabarly's domination was short-lived. Just 36 hours after the start he was back in Plymouth, one hull of the big trimaran considerably damaged. After missing one ship by only a few yards, he went below to brew some coffee and sailed into another. 'There was a tremendous crash', he said later. 'It was a small freighter and it was anchored when I ran into it at about 15 knots.' *Pen Duick IV* set out after the rest the following Tuesday, but the untried yacht was still not going well. By Wednesday Tabarly decided to retire because the boat was shaking its steering gear to pieces at speed.

The casualty list mounted rapidly. The Frenchman Joan de Kat, in his odd-looking trimaran *Yaksha,* put into Alderney for repairs. Egon Heinemann of Germany retired his *Aye-Aye* at Falmouth; Bernard

Bill Howell, the Australian who sailed four Observer races in a row, switched from a monohull to this big catamaran for 1968. She was called *Golden Cockerel* then, but later changed to *Tahiti Bill*.

Waquet's *Tamouré* sailed straight home to France: he had planned navigational help from Air France planes and they were on strike; Robert Wingate and Michael Pulsford both returned to Plymouth and scratched; Leonard Paillard broke the mast on *La Delirante*, Sandy Munro's *Ocean Highlander* also suffered a broken stick and Carozzo's *San Giorgio* limped into Falmouth with a broken rudder. The Swede William Wallin tried to come to terms with the chilly North Atlantic for five days but then decided to turn it in – he couldn't take the cold. André Foezon's *Silvia II* was also dismasted, but the Frenchman repaired her in Plymouth and set out again 12 days late – and made the crossing in an admirable 29 days.

A week after the start, it looked as though Dalling's *Voortrekker* was leading the yachts on the direct route, with Geoffrey Williams and Leslie Williams ahead of Bill Howell in the chase. To the south, Tom Follett was going well on the Azores route with *Cheers,* having covered 1,000 miles in the first seven days.

But three days later a deep depression raked the fleet and all the leaders except Geoffrey Williams lost many hours lying a-hull (all sails down) in raging seas and 60-knot winds. How did *Sir Thomas Lipton* escape? By computer. In his meticulous planning for the race, Williams had arranged for a weather centre in London to advise him by radio which course to take according to the large-scale weather pattern chart available there. The course-planners had advised him to head north as the depression approached, and while the others came to a halt, Williams was sailing away into a lead which was to prove vital. 'I think I made up perhaps 200 or 300 miles on *Golden Cockerel* and *Spirit of Cutty Sark* at this time,' he said later.

While the leaders pressed on for Newport, there were more disasters in their wake. Marc Cuiklinski's *Abrima* sank when under tow after being dismasted. Guy Piazzini retired his *Gunther III*, also with mast problems. And then came the big drama. Joan de Kat, having repaired his rig in Alderney, set off for the northern route on 9 June. Just over a week later he was sending out a Mayday signal which was picked up by an aeroplane. *Yaksha* had lost a rudder and a mast, and one float of the rickety-looking tri had come adrift, so de Kat was abandoning ship. Eventually – after a six-nation search and rescue operation – he was found by an RAF Shackleton and picked up by a Norwegian bulk carrier.

Among the leaders there were problems, too. Gliksman put *Raph* into Newfoundland with rudder troubles, and had to retire, on the day –

48

Leslie Williams, above, was a lieutenant in the Royal Navy when he entered *Spirit of Cutty Sark* for the 1968 race, and finished fourth. In 1980 the re-rigged yacht was to enter as *Kriter Lady,* with Dame Naomi James at the helm.

23 June – when the fastest yachts were getting close to Newport. On *Sir Thomas Lipton*, Geoffrey Williams had a jammed halyard which prevented him tacking away from the coast of Nova Scotia. By the time he had freed it, he was set to pass north of the Nantucket light, though the sailing instructions had been amended at the pre-race briefing to read 'to Newport, passing south of Nantucket light vessel'. Told by radio that he was taking the wrong course, Williams replied that his instructions were not amended, and asked for guidance. Colonel Odling-Smee had a hard decision to make: to make the singlehander go about and sail round the light, or let him carry on and cut the corner? He decided Williams could follow the instructions as he had them, and the Cornishman scooted home to victory across the Nantucket shoals under a 40-knot wind.

Bruce Dalling followed home in *Voortrekker* 17 hours later, sunken-eyed with fatigue after his determined chase, while Tom Follett brought *Cheers* up from the Azores route to take third place a few hours behind. Leslie Williams and Bill Howell were next in, followed by Brian Cooke, the sailing bank manager from Poole, who had made a very fast crossing of just over 34 days in a 32-footer.

Only 19 of the original 35 starters completed the course – a disappointing survival rate – and the French challenge had almost evaporated. Their first boat home was Bernard de Castelbajac in ninth position. But *Jester* reached Newport once more, albeit a full week behind the next slowest competitor. Her new owner, Michael Richey, had decided to investigate the possibilities of the southern (trade winds) route. It proved depressingly slow – he finished in 57½ days.

The race committee learned a lot from 1968: that there would have to be explicit sailing instructions to avoid a repeat of the Williams dilemma; that some sort of qualifying voyage would have to be brought in to prevent competitors setting out in untried yachts; that multihulls can be competitive (they took third, fifth and seventh places) and that the Azores route could one day provide a winner – Follett's *Cheers* had actually sailed fewer sea miles than *Sir Thomas Lipton* because she was not forced to beat into south-westerlies on the nose, as the leaders were.

There was another lesson to be learned from the 1968 race, though it can only be seen clearly in the perspective of history. Until then, the biggest boat in the fleet at the start had been first to arrive in America. That was not so in 1968 – nor was it to be in 1972, 1976 or 1980.

50

Eric Tabarly hoped his huge trimaran *Pen Duick IV* would give him a second Observer race victory, but he was forced to retire when the steering began disintegrating at speed.

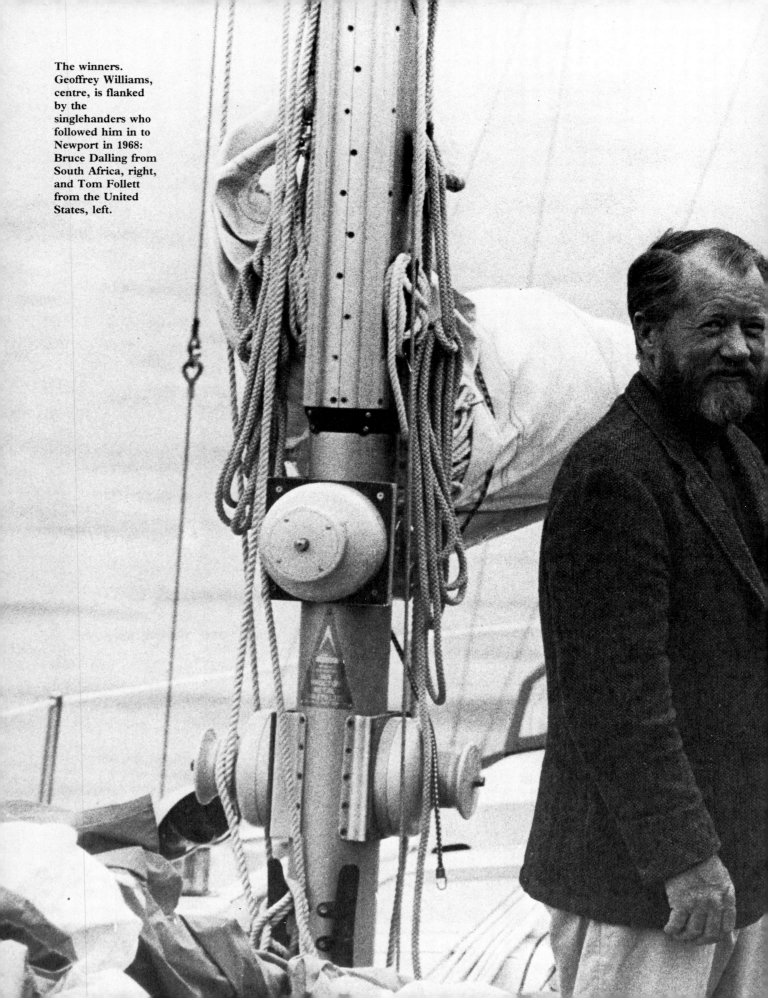

The winners.
Geoffrey Williams,
centre, is flanked
by the
singlehanders who
followed him in to
Newport in 1968:
Bruce Dalling from
South Africa, right,
and Tom Follett
from the United
States, left.

CHAPTER 5

1972—UNLUCKY FRIDAY THE 13TH

IN A SAILING BOAT, speed is a function of waterline length, so the longer the yacht is, the faster it should go. If a long hull also provides a platform for a huge sail area, then the big boat will reap a double benefit. That is why competitors in the Observer Singlehanded have sailed ever-larger yachts across the ocean, despite the constantly-voiced doubts of the pundits that the latest 'monster' was far too much for one man to handle.

There were plenty of those doubts being expressed before the start of the 1972 race, because the largest entry this time was almost twice as big as any other yacht in the fleet. It was *Vendredi 13* (Friday the 13th), a 128-foot three-masted schooner designed specially for Frenchman Jean-Yves Terlain by the American marine architect Dick Carter.

Carter's theory was that the boat would go quickly just because of her length. She would not need tall masts and huge areas of sail. So he gave her three boomed staysails; enough for a singlehanded skipper to handle comfortably without exhausting himself. Terlain was not totally convinced. Remembering the calms off the eastern coast of America which he encountered when finishing tenth four years before, he added three light genoa headsails. But it was still what Blondie Hasler described as 'a desperately inefficient rig, even to windward, with a quite excessive amount of mast and rigging for her sail area.'

But who could challenge the big schooner? Terlain's countryman Alain Colas, perhaps, in Tabarly's *Pen Duick IV* – the big trimaran which had failed in 1968 but was now ocean-tested and known to be fast. Or the young Dutchman Gerard Dijkstra in the 71-foot *Second Life*. One more impressive trimaran, *Cap 33,* was being sailed by another of the 14-strong French contingent, Jean-Marie Vidal.

That tough little American Tom Follett was back again, with another Newick-designed flier, a 46-foot trimaran called *Three Cheers*. British hopes rested on Brian Cooke, who this time had borrowed Chay Blyth's world-circling yacht *British Steel,* and Martin Minter-Kemp, now at the helm of a sleek 65-foot monohull called *Strongbow.*

It is worth noting here that the race committee had reacted against the

Dick Carter's design for the monstrous Vendredi 13 created a sensation in 1972. She went fast in a good wind, despite her inefficient rig.

The 1972 weather briefing. Around Sir Francis Chichester (with glasses, centre) were many famous names in solo sailing. Mike McMullen (back row, extreme left) stands beside Bill Howell and Brian Cooke, while Alain Colas and Jean-Yves Terlain are nearby (sixth and ninth from left, standing). The 1980 winner Phil Weld wears his *Trumpeter* sweater (standing right) as he talks to bearded Guy Hornett. Seated in front of them is Weld's countryman Tom Follett (extreme right). Teresa Remiszewska, the Polish woman skipper, sits in the sun, fourth from the left.

blatant commercial names of the 1968 race and forbidden obvious sponsor-inspired boat titles. Yet *Strongbow* (from the Bulmers cider makers) was let through the noose, as were *Second Life* (the name of a margarine in Holland), *British Steel,* allowed to keep the title because she was so famous, and *Cap 33* (a French beer). By contrast, one of the French girl sailors, Anne Michailof, arrived in a yacht called *Pieter Stuyvesant,* explaining that it commemorated the famous mayor of New York, not the cigarette. The committee members were not impressed – the name had to be changed to *P.S.*

Anne was one of three women singlehanders in the race, but none of them attracted as much attention from the reporters and photographers in

Plymouth as the oldest man in the race. He was Sir Francis Chichester, returning to the scene of his earlier triumph after missing the 1968 race, with his latest *Gipsy Moth*, number V. She measured 57 feet and was a powerful boat, but the 70-year-old skipper looked very frail and there was some doubt about his ability to handle her.

It was a cosmopolitan fleet which gathered in Millbay before the start on Saturday 17 June. There were a dozen countries represented, with Czechoslovakia and Poland sending entries from behind the Iron Curtain for the first time. The multihull proportion had dropped sharply – just six trimarans and two catamarans this time. But the age and size range of the yachts was the widest yet.

Sir Francis Chichester takes his leave of lady Chichester and their son Giles, just before the 1972 start, left. But his race was not to last long, for the mizzen mast of *Gipsy Moth V* was critically damaged in a collision with a ship, right.

At least there was wind for the start. A brisk south-westerly hustled the fleet away when the gun sounded at noon, and the French were quickly providing most of the front runners. Marc Linski sailed his *Isles du Frioul* away like the star of a dinghy fleet; the only trouble was that he had crossed the line before the gun. Terlain kept the massive *Vendredi 13* down to leeward and eased her through the froth of spectator boats with splendid coolness. Colas kept well clear of the mad melee at the start, while Tom Follett planned to go through the eastern end of the breakwater with *Three Cheers*, until he found it so blocked with spectator craft that he was forced to tack away and follow the rest. Phil Weld sped past the big French schooner in his trimaran *Trumpeter* and Mike McMullen followed him with his 32-foot sloop *Binkie II*. They were all names which were to become familiar in the expanding legend of the Observer Singlehanded.

But as the leaders headed off for the Eddystone light and the Lizard, the spectators were concerned at the slow progress of Sir Francis Chichester in *Gipsy Moth V*. He had sailed over the line after most of the rest and then headed in dangerously close to Penlee Point, only tacking away when he was within a few yards of running on to the rocks. Then we could see that his big jib had become wrapped around the forestay and there was an air of desperate weariness about the way he went forward to sort out the mess. Before the start there had been reports of the old navigator having an infection of the bone marrow and needing transfusions to restore the proper balance in the blood. Watching his struggle to get the big ketch going that Saturday, I wondered whether he was wise to set out on such a voyage at all.

Later that day I flew over Mounts Bay to pick up the leaders as they scudded off into what was now a strong south-westerly. There was *Vendredi*, crashing her way through the lengthening rollers, having averaged 15 knots since the start. Not far behind was Joel Charpentier's *Wild Rocket*, rocketing along rather wildly with what looked like too much sail up. Sure enough, she blew out some sails that evening and had to return to Plymouth for repairs.

Also quickly back in port was the Belgian Oscar Debra: the fuel tank on his *Olva II* had split and disgorged diesel oil all over his food and equipment. Poor Oscar; he had planned to enter but missed the 1968 race, quickly retired from the 1972 and 1976 races and was not to have the joy of sailing over the line at Newport until 1980 – but he made it in the end. On

Jean-Yves Terlain, left, and his rival Alain Colas, right, met in the middle of the Atlantic when the 1972 race was ten days old — an incredible coincidence in millions of square miles of ocean.

the Sunday after the race started he watched the last two yachts get away – Wolf Kirchner's *White Dolphin* from Germany and Teresa Remiszewska's *Komodor* from Poland. That made up the 54 starters of the 1972 race. Exactly 40 of them were to make the crossing to Newport inside the 60-day time limit set this time.

One reason for that high success rate had to be the weather. In 1972 the conditions were kindly most of the way across the ocean, though there was one brisk gale which quickly passed through the fleet on 1 July. Most of the singlehanders arriving in Newport complained about the calms and fogs experienced near the American coast rather than of the bad weather. There was nothing to compare with the crucial gale of the 1968 race, and most of the fleet could keep sailing all the way across, whether the skipper had chosen the direct route or the Azores way, below the Gulf Stream. In fact, the yachts had split sides of the course soon after the start, with Colas and Terlain taking their big boats the direct route, followed by Minter-Kemp in *Strongbow* and Gerard Dijkstra in *Second Life*. To the south, Bill Howell had elected to take the Azores route for the first time and made good progress, followed by Jean-Marie Vidal in *Cap 33*.

But the sharp gale on 1 July disrupted the pattern. Dijkstra lost his mast that day and had to be towed to St John's Newfoundland. Bob Miller, the sailing band leader, also lost his stick; his *Mersea Pearl* did not survive – it sank when under tow. Murray Sayle, the second Australian entrant, was luckier. He lost the mast on his big cruising catamaran *Lady of Fleet* later in the race but was towed safely into Newport by an American coastguard vessel. His compatriot, Bill Howell, also failed to finish. After making a very good passage on the southern route he collided with a Russian trawler in the fog near the American coast. He would probably have been fifth home.

The saddest disaster story of the whole race was that of *Gipsy Moth V*. Sir Francis Chichester had decided to give up the race within a week of the start. On 24 June he started to head back to Plymouth, but some confusion arose; his reports and the message he tried to pass back to an RAF Nimrod aircraft were misinterpreted and a full rescue operation was mounted. Then a French weather ship, hoping to help out the old mariner, actually came too close and broke *Gipsy Moth's* mizzen mast, so that she would be very difficult to get back home. Eventually, *HMS Salisbury*, a British Navy frigate, went out to the yacht and transferred Sir Francis's son Giles, a

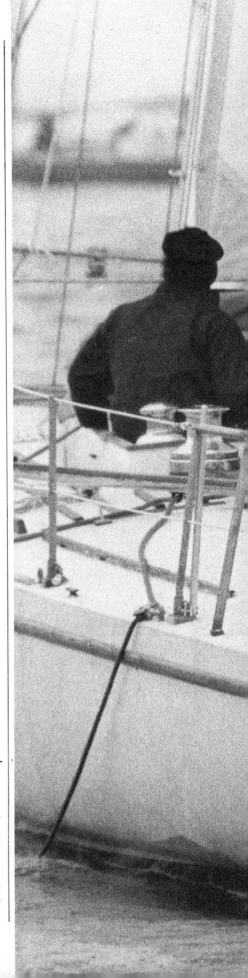

Martin Minter-Kemp's *Strongbow* was a long, slim and swift 65-footer, specially designed for the race by Paul Weychan.

friend and a rigging expert aboard. Later an expert yachtsman also joined the boat and helped to sail her back home. Sadly, after the French weather ship left *Gipsy Moth V* she collided with an American yacht which was also trying to find and help the singlehander. The boat sank and seven lives were lost, a tragic end to a chapter of misplaced well-intentions. It turned out to be Sir Francis's last voyage; he died before the year was out.

But among the leaders there were no disasters – just the strangest coincidence. Alain Colas in *Pen Duick IV* was about half-way across the Atlantic by 27 June, surmising that he must be either in the lead or close to the front boat, for he had kept up a fast average dispite losing his self-steering gear four days after the start. Then, two miles ahead, he suddenly made out the unmistakable profile of *Vendredi 13*. Coaxing a little extra speed out of his huge craft, Colas edged *Pen Duick* past the big schooner by 3.40 in the afternoon. 'Passed Terlain and celebrated by eating a tin of home-made peaches in syrup,' he wrote in his log.

It was to be a lead that he never lost. Despite the calms towards the end of the passage, Colas arrived off Newport in the afternoon of Friday 7 July. That morning an Observer photographer and I had reconnoitred the whole of Newport Sound and the area around Nantucket Light by aeroplane. We found only *Vendredi 13*, inching along in minimal wind, with Terlain stretched out under a sunshade. He might have been trying harder if he had realised that Colas and the big trimaran were scuttling on to the finish. In fact, Colas finished that evening to take nearly 5½ days off Geoffrey Williams's record, and Terlain had to be content with second place 16 hours behind.

Jean-Marie Vidal brought *Cap 33* up from the Azores route to take third place a full three days later, and Brian Cooke was the first British skipper home with the Chay Blyth ketch *British Steel* in just under 25 days. All of them had broken the old record, but thereafter the finishers were spread out. Tom Follett was a disappointed fifth, complaining of having hit every hole in the wind possible, and Martin Minter-Kemp brought *Strongbow* home in seventh place with considerable structural damage. Perhaps the most impressive performance of all, after Colas's victory, was Alain Gliksman's eighth place, and the trophy for first boat home under 35 feet, with the little converted lake day sailer *Toucan*. A frail, wet and frighteningly uncomfortable boat, she had been driven hard all the way to finish in 28½ days.

1976–THE MAJESTIC MISTAKE

THE 1976 OBSERVER SINGLEHANDED was, in some respects, the high water mark of the race. It had the biggest fleet and the biggest boats of the series. It also sailed through some of the fiercest weather experienced in the North Atlantic by any of the Observer race fleets. But in the perspective of history it is probable that the 1976 Singlehanded will be remembered more for its big boats than anything else.

Of those, the real monster was Alain Colas's gigantic *Club Méditerranée*. Though he had beaten Terlain's three-master in 1972, the ambitious Colas had been impressed by the huge monohull. But a mere 128 foot in length and three masts was not enough for Colas: his designer conceived a yacht nearly twice as big. The result was a staggering sailing machine – 236 feet long from stem to stern, powered by clouds of sail spread over four masts, littered with sophisticated navigation and control gear, including a satellite navigation system, television cameras to monitor the sails on each mast, the latest in radar, long-distance radio, weather information systems and even air-conditioning for the skipper's control centre and deckhouse.

As if all that were not amazing enough, Colas had pushed through the financing and building of this incredible boat when all but the most intensely-committed man would have given up in despair. For in the spring of 1975 he had suffered a grievous injury that nearly caused his leg to be amputated. The anchor chain of *Manureva* (new name for *Pen Duick IV,* used when Colas sailed her round the world singlehanded) became caught around his right leg and almost severed it. But the fiercely-determined Colas did not hesitate; he continued working on the project from his hospital bed and eventually the 'cathedral of sails' as he liked to call it, was completed. It was late, of course, and the Frenchman had some difficulty in convincing the race committee that he was physically fit enough to manage such a huge craft. But at last the special qualifying voyages and preliminaries were over and the stately four-masted schooner glided into Millbay to dominate the assembled fleet like a king amongst commoners.

Some of those commoners were impressive in their own right, just the

Club Méditerránee — 236 feet of sailing sophistication.

While the hundreds of spectators boats swarmed around the big four-master, Tabarly swung *Pen Duick VI* over on to port tack (left foreground) and began to build up a lead which would prove crucial.

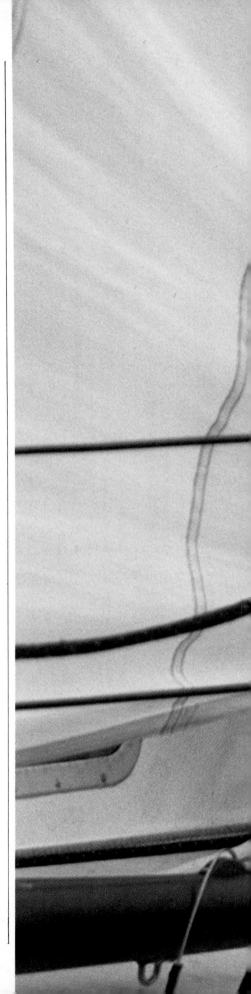

Clare Francis was not going to be short of things to do on the voyage. As she sailed out of Plymouth she was committed to radio reports to a daily newspaper, as well as shooting film for a BBC television documentary.

same. *Vendredi* was back, for example, though this time renamed *ITT Oceanic* and entered in the name of another tough Frenchman, Yvon Fauconnier. Her first skipper, Jean-Yves Terlain, had taken over the 70-foot catamaran which Robin Knox-Johnston had used to win the 1974 Round Britain Race with Gerry Boxall. She too was retitled – *British Oxygen* became *Kriter III*. (The rule about sponsors' names had been relaxed and they brought about some odd titlings throughout the fleet).

And the old master was back. Eric Tabarly entered his world-girdling racing ketch *Pen Duick VI*, taking her out to do his solo qualifying cruise while the Whitbread Round the World Race fleet was stopping over at Rio de Janeiro. Originally he had hoped to sail his revolutionary hydrofoil trimaran, but she could not be built in time, so he elected to go in the big racer which is normally crewed by some 18 men.

Could anyone challenge the French contingent, which looked stronger than ever this time? The Americans had a couple of likely front runners in Tom Grossman (who had bought Vidal's *Cap 33* trimaran after the 1972 race) and Mike Kane in a 62-foot trimaran called *Spirit of America*. Sadly, Phil Weld's 60-foot trimaran *Gulf Streamer* would not be in the list – she had capsized on the way across the Atlantic for the start. British hopes rested largely on the shoulders of Mike McMullen, the tough ex-Marine Commando officer who took over Tom Follett's *Three Cheers* after the 1972 race and had proved her speed two years later by coming second to *British Oxygen* in the Round Britain Race. And David Palmer, a sailing journalist, was intent on doing well with his 35-foot trimaran *FT*. But the French seemed to have daunting strength in depth, and it looked as though they could easily mop up all the trophies. There were more of them this time, because the race committee had split the fleet into three classes – Pen Duick for the biggest boats; Gipsy Moth for the intermediates and Jester for the small ones – up to 38 foot overall.

At the start, each class had a separate gun, with 30 minutes between them. It had to be so because the armada that set out that Saturday 5 June totalled no less than 125 yachts of all shapes and sizes, with four of them sailed by women, including the first British woman singlehander – Clare Francis in her 38-foot *Robertson's Golly*.

A fair breeze helped the racers away through the now-expected compress of craft heavily laden with spectators. Colas sailed his stately schooner through them all to a well-timed start, but it was obvious that he couldn't

Jean-Yves Terlain
began the race at
the helm of the 70
foot catamaran
Kriter III, which
had won the 1974
Round Britain
Race as *British
Oxygen.* The
powerful cat was
not to survive the
voyage, though her
skipper was
recovered safely.

have hoisted all the sail himself – his helpers were aboard until just before
the ten-minute gun. 'What would happen if he had sail problems?' was the
obvious question being asked.

So the 125 of them went away into what showed on the weather map as a
series of deep depressions scurrying across the Atlantic: it promised to be a
hard ride. After three hours Tabarly had taken a significant lead, from
Mike Kane in the American trimaran, with *Three Cheers* up to third place,
despite starting 30 minutes behind the others. The monster? She wasn't
seen, but everyone knew she must be moving along implacably as the
south-westerlies increased. It seemed inevitable that her sheer size would
prove overpowering, particularly when the first couple of weeks of the race
produced a whole series of gales. Opinions varied when the post mortems
were held in Newport, but most skippers reckoned that the Great Circle
route had meant sailing through seven full gales, and those yachts towards
the northern extremity had been in storm-force winds.

Inevitably there were plenty of casualties. The eventual tally was 51
boats retired, sunk or not arrived by the time the span of the race ran
out – 50 days this year. In the early weeks the most dramatic casualties were
Tony Bullimore's trimaran *Toria,* which caught fire and sank, and
Dominique Berthier's sloop *5100,* which also sank after being in a collision.
Luckily, there were merchant ships close at hand in both cases and the
skippers were quickly rescued.

The second week of gales saw the retirement list grow rapidly to more
than 30 yachts, many with damaged self-steering gear and quite a number
with rigging problems. Pierre Fehlmann's *Gauloises* began to take water
and he was saved by a container ship in desperately dangerous conditions;
Angus Primrose's *Demon Demo* was capsized and dismasted – he sailed her
home calmly under jury rig; Jean-Yves Terlain's big catamaran broke her
beams in the big seas and he had to be saved by Russian fishermen.

Meanwhile, out in mid-ocean, even the favourites were having troubles.
The self-steering gear on Tabarly's big ketch was damaged beyond repair
when he was just about 1,000 miles out. It was 1964 all over again. But this
time he was so tired, and it seemed so unlikely that he could now get to

The American
singlehander Tom
Grossman was fifth
to finish, though
only two days
slower than
Jean-Marie Vidal's
crossing with the
same trimaran in
much easier
conditions four
years earlier.

Centre. The 38-foot
Robertson's Golly
(Clare Francis)
established a new
woman's record of
just under 29 days
and two hours —
and arrived in time
for the 4 July
celebrations.
Right. *Jester* failed
to reach America
for the first time in
the race's history.
Skipper Michael
Richey opted out to
sail round Ireland
instead.

Newport ahead of the rest, that he turned away south-east for about a day 'to give myself time to rest and think' he said later. 'Then I decided that I could carry on after all and turned west again. It was hard, but it was possible.'

A fateful decision, because at that time Tabarly could not have known that Colas's monster four-master was shedding halyards with monotonous regularity. It soon became clear to Colas that he could not complete the crossing without repair, so he headed off to St John's, Newfoundland, for a stop-over that was to destroy the hopes he had built around his 'cathedral.'

At the end of the third week of the race, when the record time set by Colas in 1972 had come and gone, there was still no sign of a winner at Newport. The raking storms of the first fortnight had given way to debilitating calms and fogs, and rumours were rife in the finishing port. Various schools favoured Tabarly, Grossman, McMullen or Bill Howell, while everyone knew that Colas was on his way down the coast from Newfoundland and could still snatch the glory.

Then Gerard Pestey, a French sailor who had been in the 1972 race and was in Newport with his big cruising trimaran to watch the finish, looked out of his hatch in the dawn and recognised a big black ketch with one man aboard, milling up and down Newport Harbour waiting for somebody to realise that he was there. It was Tabarly, who had crept in during the night without using his radio. Despite the loss of his self-steering and the punishing demands of the big ketch's massive sails, he had completed the course in under 24 days, even counting the day lost sailing the wrong way. Wasn't it exhausing? 'Oh no', he replied with a gentle smile, 'it is just a question of muscles'. He pronounced it 'mooscles'. But the sunken eyes and deeply-etched fatigue lines told the real story of his race: it had cost him a bone-wracking weariness and dug deep into his resources of stamina and determination. In retrospect, it might well have been the most demanding test in a life that has been crowded with challenges. Colas arrived in the monster seven hours behind his old mentor, the wound of finishing second salted by the race committee's decision to penalise him 58 hours for having more than the allowed assistance at St John's.

Then came the most astonishing event of the 1976 race – Mike Birch, the Canadian yacht delivery skipper who lives in England, scooted in with his little 31-foot Val trimaran, *The Third Turtle*, to take third place overall, victory in the Jester class, the multihull handicap prize and the newly-

Guy Hornett sailed a totally different yacht in 1976. After the small, bilge-keeled *Blue Smoke* of 1972, he transferred to a big trimaran called *Old Moore's Almanack*. She took the skipper to America nearly five days more quickly than his 1972 passage.

donated Lizzie McMullen trophy for the first multihull to Newport. She crossed the line a little over a day behind the winner and only 17 hours behind the schooner which had cost about 60 times as much and weighed 176 times the displacement of the tiny tri. *Club Méditerránee* had turned out to be a majestic mistake. Birch, the archetypal modest man, shrugged off his astounding feat and insisted that he had slept five hours each night and not pushed hard. But Walter Greene, a strong and experienced racing yachtsman from America, who sailed a similar Val trimaran into eighth place nearly three days later, said: 'He's a hard man. He must have been driving her all the way.' Only three hours behind Birch came the second surprise — Kazimierz Jaworski of Poland finished fourth in his 38-foot monohull *Spaniel,* which he had designed himself. Again, it was clear that the boat had been sailed skilfully and with total commitment all the way across the ocean, gales or no gales. Utter fatigue showed in every line of Jaworski's crumpled face.

After them came the more expected front runners — Grossman in fifth place; Jean-Claude Parisis of France to take the Gipsy Moth honours and David Palmer, first Briton home, with the pink-painted *FT*. Clare Francis shattered the record for a woman singlehander's fastest crossing set by Marie-Claude Fauroux four years earlier. She finished in just over 29 days to take 13th place overall, while Geoffrey Hales picked up the monohull handicap trophy for getting a cruising Rival 34 sloop to Newport in 32½ days.

And McMullen? He simply disappeared. After that early sighting, three hours after the race began, there was no sign of the skipper or his bright yellow trimaran until just before the 1980 race began, when a small piece of wreckage was discovered off Iceland. It seems he had taken a far northerly course and somehow come to grief well away from normal search and rescue areas. It was a particularly tragic end to a whole-hearted and courageous life, for his wife Lizzie had died the week before the race, electrocuted while helping him to prepare *Three Cheers*.

Also lost in this race was Mike Flanagan, a British-born sailor who had made his home in the United States. His specially-designed 38-footer *Galloping Gael,* had been one of the favourites for the Jester class honours. It was found in mid-Atlantic with no sign of the skipper; it seemed that he had probably fallen off the boat. These two deaths were the first in the 16-year history of the Observer Singlehanded.

The huge demands of victory in the storm-tossed 1976 race are written clearly in the haggard face and sunken eyes of Eric Tabarly aboard *Pen Duick VI*. Behind them, the more serene features of the tall ships gathered at Newport for the American bi-centenary celebrations.

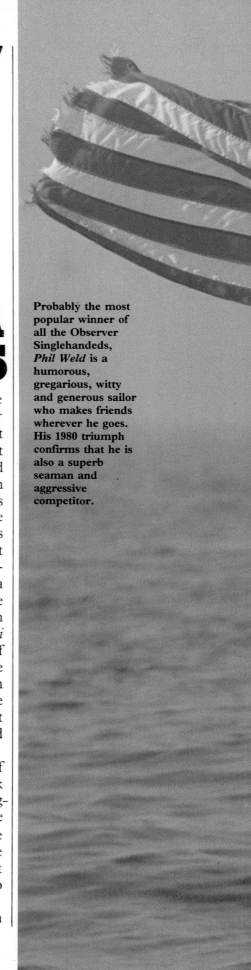

CHAPTER 7

1980—AMERICA VICTORIOUS

AT THE PARIS BOAT SHOW in January 1977, there was a 'round table discussion' organised by the news magazine *Le Point* about the Observer Singlehanded Race for 1980. The Royal Western Yacht Club had just issued the new rules and conditions for the race, and the French were not well pleased. For the Race Committee had decided that this child it had nurtured with such loving care was in danger of growing into an uncontrollable monster. There had always been discussions — perhaps arguments is the more accurate word — among yachtsmen about the delights and dangers of sending a huge fleet of singlehanded boats across the Atlantic. Some thought it criminal, because solo sailors clearly cannot obey the basic law for the avoidance of collision at sea — to keep a look-out at all times. Others contended that it was an acceptable risk for a singlehander to chance being run down by a ship, as long as he was the one in danger and he would not threaten other lives. Obviously that distinction became more important with the arrival of such monster yachts as *Vendredi* and *Club Méditerranée.* Most of the transatlantic boats would come off second best in a collision with a Grand Banks trawler, for example, but the huge four-master was big enough and powerful enough to plough through a fishing fleet causing untold damage — and possibly death. So in 1976 the committee took two important decisions: to limit the size of the 1980 fleet to a maximum of 110 yachts; and to stipulate that none of them should measure more than 56 feet overall.

In Paris there were cries of despair and accusations of perfidy. Some of the Continental singlehanders were convinced that it was all a plot to break the French domination of the event. It wasn't, of course. Jack Odling-Smee, the race committee chairman, put it quite simply: 'We have amended the rules for three reasons. First, we do not want to be a menace to other shipping in the Channel. Second, we want to make sure that more yachts actually reach the other end of the course, and third, we have set class limits to try to adhere to the original concept of the race — which is to defeat the ocean rather than the other competitors.'

There were some very disappointed singlehanders who had been

Probably the most popular winner of all the Observer Singlehandeds, *Phil Weld* is a humorous, gregarious, witty and generous sailor who makes friends wherever he goes. His 1980 triumph confirms that he is also a superb seaman and aggressive competitor.

The brilliantly-striped mainsail of Riguidel's trimaran *VSD* makes her instantly recognisable in the melee round the start boat as the 1980 fleet gets away. Most yachts took the inner, favoured end of the line, but few made as good a start as Michael Richey and the little *Jester* (square sail, extreme left of picture).

planning monster yachts for 1980. Pierre Fehlmann of Switzerland had a larger version of the fragile *Gauloises* on the drawing board; Jacques Timsit of France had a big boat under way and the American Phil Weld was doubly disappointed. Having missed the 1976 race because his *Gulf Streamer* was capsized, he had pushed ahead with a near-replica — also measuring 60 feet overall — to be sailed in 1980. Now it looked as though he would miss the race again, because although *Rogue Wave*, as she was to be called, could be shortened to 56 feet overall, the design could not be modified enough to fit the other parameter — 46 feet on the waterline. Alain Colas stated bluntly that he would not go in such a race.

But some other solo skippers were not too displeased with the new limit. Gerry Dijkstra, the Dutchman who had made a fast crossing in 1976 with his 56-foot *Bestevaer* (once he had been back to Plymouth for repairs to the rig) thought the new rule would suit him and his boat admirably. The British sailor Don Clark was already planning a 56-footer, and the speedy Pole Kazimierz Jaworski, was working on a similar-size craft. And there was always that extraordinary hydrofoil trimaran that Eric Tabarly had been planning before the 1976 race. Now it could well turn out to be a hot favourite for 1980 — and fast enough to beat the record, size limit or no.

As the months passed the cries of anguish died and the news of potential front runners with new boats proliferated. In 1978 the French organised their own — unlimited — solo race across the Atlantic, from St Malo to Guadeloupe. It was called the Route du Rhum and turned out to be a battle between Michel Malinovsky from France in a big, sleek monohull and the modest Canadian Mike Birch in the 38-foot trimaran which Walter Green had designed, build and sailed to fourth place in that year's Round Britain double-handed Race. In a palpitating finish, Birch crossed the line first with just 90 seconds to spare after 4,000 miles of sailing. It proved that his outstanding performance in the Observer Singlehanded was no flash in the pan.

Third in the Route du Rhum was the ebullient Phil Weld, as he had been in the Round Britain Race. *Rogue Wave* was proving fast and manageable, and Weld let slip that he just *might* build a smaller version to fit the rule for the 1980 Observer race.

The great sadness of the Route du Rhum was that Alain Colas, competing with the old *Manureva*, disappeared as tragically and as mystifyingly as McMullen had two years before. The intensely-

Left. Marc Pajot took over the helm of *Paul Ricard*, after Eric Tabarly was forced to withdraw by a shoulder injury. but he was not an official competitor and his finish among the leaders in Newport will not go in the race records.

Below. Tom Grossman was made favourite by the bookmakers when Tabarly withdrew, but his speedy trimaran *Kriter VII* lost an irredeemable 26½ hours when it collided with the Spanish entry *Garuda* minutes before the start.

Nick Keig's *Three Legs of Mann III* went very swiftly, although he said she was built more for family cruising than transatlantic race winning.

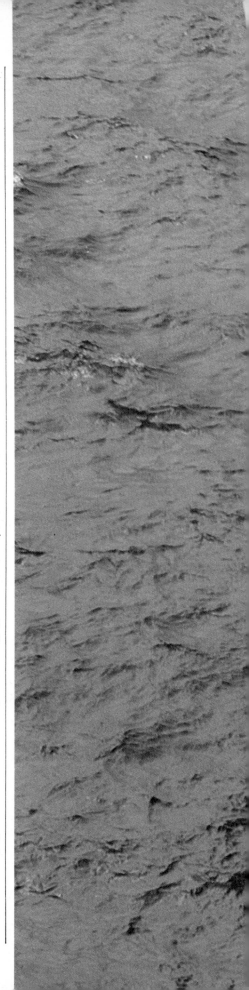

The Italian doctor Edoard Austoni sailed a magnificent race in his elegant *Chica Boba II*, despite damaging two fingers in the mainsail halyard winch soon after the start.

competitive world of single- and short-handed sailing could ill afford to lose two such powerful protagonists within such a short span.

In the early months of 1979, as the October qualifying date for the 1980 race came nearer, the likely favourites began to emerge. Tabarly had indeed entered his new trimaran, now called *Paul Ricard*. Weld had also built his scaled-down version of *Rogue Wave*, and called her *Moxie*. Mike Birch had another Dick Newick design in the list — a version of the famous *Three Cheers* 46-footer, to be called *Olympus Photo*. Jaworski's new 56-footer was called *Spaniel II*, and Tom Grossman was planning a new maxi-size trimaran — again to Newick's design.

The British challenge seemed to revolve around the skippers who had finished first and second in the '78 Round Britain Race. Chay Blyth entered his winning *Great Britain IV*, but later dropped out because of lack of sponsorship funds. Nick Keig, second in the Round Britain, had sold his fast *Three Legs of Mann II* and built another, slightly heavier and roomier version of the Derek Kelsall design called *Three Legs of Mann III*.

It certainly looked a very competitive fleet, with a strong contingent from the United States. Backing Weld and Grossman were Walter Greene in another of his own trimaran designs, *Chaussettes Olympia;* Philip Steggall in a similar yacht called *Jeans Foster;* and Warren Luhrs in a 54-foot monohull called *Tuesday's Child*. Not to be discounted were the Italian Edoardo Austoni in his big mono called *Chica Boba II* and Bertie Reed, from South Africa, who entered the old but still competitive *Voortrekker* which Bruce Dalling had sailed into second place back in 1968.

Against them were ranged the daunting ranks of French yachtsmen, many of them Tabarly disciples and just as tough. Dijkstra's *Bestevaer* had been taken over by Oliver de Kersauson and renamed *Kriter VI;* Jean-Pierre Millet had a strong-looking 52-foot monohull called *Open Space* and there were fast trimarans entered by Eugene Riguidel, Alain Labbe, Eric Loizeau and Michel Horeau (the old *Cap 33*, now christened *Maurice Lidchi Enterprises* – such are the sacrifices of sponsorship). Also not to be overlooked was the sleek 44-foot monohull of Daniel Gilard, a likely contender for honours in the Gipsy Moth class, which this time took in boats up to 44 feet overall.

So despite the size limit, the 1980 race was building up to be a fiercely-disputed competition, with lots of good incidental stories for the media men. To start with, there were the four women sailors. Dame Naomi

James, the New Zealander who had been the first woman to sail round the world singlehanded by the classic route, had entered the same boat, now called *Kriter Lady*. Florence Arthaud, the darling of the French reporters and cameramen after her strong performance in the Route du Rhum, was down to go in her 49-footer *Miss Dubonnet*. Judy Lawson, a dinghy-racing expert from America, was to helm a fast 32-footer called *Serta Perfectsleeper* and Joan Connors, also American, was to be the first grandmother ever in the race. (Sadly, she never made it to the start).

As if all that were not enough to keep any features editor happy, Dame Naomi's husband Rob was also in the lists. It was the first time there had ever been a husband and wife race within the race. But the best news of all for the newsmen came in November 1979, when The Observer announced that it had arranged for every yacht to be fitted with an Argos system transponder, so that everyone following the race would know exactly where each boat was all the way across the ocean.

The Argos system is a world-wide operational weather data collection satellite system which has evolved out of the co-operative space programme developed by the United States and France, involving the American National Aeronautics and Space Administration (NASA), the National Oceanic and Atmospheric Administration (NOAA) and the French Centre National d'Etudes Spatiales (CNES).

The transponders fitted to each of the competing boats would send automatic signals 500 miles into space, to be collected and stored by the Tiros-N and NOAA-6 satellites, circling the globe on polar orbits. The messages would be 'read out' once each orbit to three ground telemetry stations — one in France and two in the United States. The information would then be sent to a processing centre in Washington, from there to Toulouse for decoding, and on to race information centres in Britain, France and America. The computer print-out in those centres would show the exact location of each yacht, the direction it was sailing and the progress made since the last 'sighting'. It was to be a highly-complex operation, with data being passed on through various companies of the Honeywell computer organisation, particularly Cii Honeywell Bull, the French subsidiary. The British Meteorological Office was to receive some of the data, which could help it to make more accurate weather forecasts during the race, and in turn the BBC's World Service was to broadcast a weather bulletin specially prepared for the singlehanders at 3 a.m. Greenwich time each day.

Left. Police sergeant Peter Phillips raised £2,000 for children's charities in his native Exeter area, despite the fact that his trimaran *Livery Dole* broke up and was lost in mid-Atlantic.

Below. Canadian skipper Michael Birch reckoned he was out of the running when a large section of the bridge deck on his trimaran *Olympus Photo* was broken away by the constant pounding of the ocean. But he completed a makeshift repair and pushed on to finish fourth.

The great benefit of the Argos system, quite apart from giving a complete record of where every boat was at every stage of the race, was that it would pinpoint any search and rescue operation. If a singlehanded skipper was in difficulties, he could operate a special switch on his transponder which would change the routine message to an emergency signal. Any rescue operation could be directed accurately to the yachtsman in trouble, because the satellite would give an exact 'fix'. In dire emergency, the skipper could also unship the transponder and take it with him into the life-raft. Truly, the space age had come to the Observer Singlehanded.

Obviously, the cost of such a system is considerable — it worked out at about £1,000 for each competing yacht. The Observer was able to cover this through a collaboration with Europe 1, the leading commercial radio station in France, which became a joint-sponsor of the event and used the Argos system information to broadcast regular bulletins on the race across Europe.

The time required to instal the transponders on each yacht meant that the committee needed the boats in Millbay Dock earlier than usual. They had to be 'on parade' by Friday 30 May, eight days before the start. A few did not make it and incurred time penalties. Others who had seemed certain to go when the list was closed just could not get their boats to England. So Joan Connors dropped out, as did Jean Lacombe, a veteran of the first two races who had planned to make his reappearance in 1980.

The biggest disappointment was the withdrawal of Eric Tabarly. A few weeks before the start the race committee heard from France that although the extensive alterations to *Paul Ricard* were all on schedule, her skipper was not fit. An old skiing injury restricted movement in one shoulder and he could not raise his right arm above shoulder level. Clearly he would not be able to hoist sails or cope with many other tasks on board, so he had to scratch. His sponsors asked if Marc Pajot — the former dinghy racing champion who had been Tabarly's partner in the 1979 French double-handed race to Bermuda and back — could take over the entry. But according to the rules Pajot had not completed his qualifying cruise in the boat at the right time, so it could not be. Instead it was agreed that *Paul Ricard* could sail in the race with Pajot at the helm, but he would be an unofficial entrant and not eligible for any trophies. The boat would carry an Argos transponder. 'It makes no difference,' said a French yachting

Judith Lawson is a brave American woman sailor who has lots of experience in small boats. Her race in the 1980 Observer Singlehanded came to an end when *Serta Perfectsleeper* was dismasted off Newfoundland.

journalist. 'If Marc is first to Newport the world will say he won La Transat.'

Similarly, Jean-Yves Terlain came to Plymouth in his startling new catamaran *Gautier I* and asked if he could be a late entry. In fairness to all those who had conformed with the rules, the committee had to turn him down — sadly, because it was Terlain's fourth successive Observer Singlehanded. However, he too was allowed to start as an unofficial entry and his odd-looking craft was fitted with a transponder.

The morning of Saturday 7 June dawned bright though cloudy, with a freshening breeze from the south-west to get the armada of 88 yachts away from the start line just outside the breakwater across Plymouth Sound. There was an almost palpable tension in the air as the dock gates opened and the most varied fleet in the history of competitive sailing crept out into the Sound in preparation for the off. The first drama came a full 2½ hours before the start. Florence Arthaud's beamy racer *Miss Dubonnet* had caused some frowns among the scrutineers; they suggested that her rigging was

Top left. Chris Smith sailed *Sadler Bluejacket,* one of the smallest boats in the race, at just 25 feet overall. Below, left. Philip Steggall was third man home and first in the *Gipsy Moth* class with his trimaran *Jeans Foster.* Right. The American skipper Warren Luhrs was forced to retire his graceful sloop *Tuesday's Child* when her keel problems proved insuperable.

Below. Walter
Greene designed,
built and sailed the
trimaran
*Chaussettes
Olympia* into fifth
place to make it
three out of the
first five for
America.

rather lightweight for the Atlantic and that it could be beefed up. So a
party of her helpers worked most of the night before the start renewing the
rig — just in case. It proved a tragic mistake. As soon as *Miss Dubonnet* was
out into clear water and Florence hoisted her mainsail, the wind filled it, a
new but 'soft' bottlescrew collapsed as it came under strain and the mast
snapped at the lower spreaders. With a sickening crack, the rig collapsed
about the boat, and the distraught skipper collapsed just as
comprehensively into tears.

Even then, the pre-start dramas were not over. Tom Grossman's fast
trimaran *Kriter VII* — favourite in the bookmaker's lists after *Paul Ricard*
dropped out — also came to grief. Grossman was zipping up and down the
line with a mass of sail set as the seconds ticked away to the gun. He

Jacques Timsit was
going well when his
yacht *Motorola* was
holed by some
floating wreckage
and quickly sank.
He was soon
rescued.

ducked below for a moment to pick up his stopwatch and his yacht
careered into the 48-foot *Garuda*, sailed by the Spanish skipper Victor
Sagi. The big tri rode up on to the mono, scattering life lines as it went.
Garuda was able to continue, but *Kriter VII's* starboard float was holed
and Grossman had no choice but to head back to Mashford's Yard for
repairs.

On the stroke of 2 pm the Royal Navy's gun boomed out and they were
away. Young Alain Labbe sustained the French tradition of a fast start by
steering his little trimaran *Hydrofolie* over the line first, with Pajot
powering after him in *Paul Ricard* – cheeky that, for the race committee
had asked the unofficial racers to keep clear of the rest at the start. The
conditions were perfect for the multihulls and they were soon setting the
pace as the fleet moved swiftly away towards the Eddystone light.
Riguidel's *VSD* was going quickly but well off the wind. Weld's *Moxie*, by
contrast, was both fast and close-winded – she left the light to port where
most of the others had to go round it. So *Moxie* soon established a lead,
with Eric Loizeau's *Gauloises IV* and Birch's *Olympus Photo* close behind
and Nick Keig following up with *Three Legs*.

When the first satellite-observed positions came through later that day, it
was the unofficial boat *Paul Ricard* which had covered the greatest
distance, with Weld, Loizeau, Birch, Keig and Steggall top of the order in
the official lists. All were trimarans. In the husband and wife battle, Rob
James's *Boatfile* had benefited from an astute early tack and he was close
up to that leading pack. Naomi was going well, but at a more sedate pace
further back.

The first week of the race proved to be full of incident and astonishing
progress. The map which The Observer published eight days after the
start showed the leading boats, as tracked by the Argos system, close to 35
degrees west — almost half-way across the ocean and set for a record-
shattering passage. It happened because the winds, unusually, blew from
the north all that week and almost every yacht was on its fastest point of
sailing. The trimarans loved it — *Paul Ricard* was still setting the pace and
the official fleet was headed alternately by *Moxie* and *VSD*, both covering
more than 200 miles each day. Also close up were *Three Legs* and Greene's
Chaussettes Olympia. Eric Loizeau's *Gauloises IV* had also been snapping
at the leaders' heels through the first week, but at the end of it she slowed
and turned away — the continuous pounding at speed into the Atlantic

The first-ever husband and wife duel in the race was won convincingly by Robert James, who finished 16th in his small Val class trimaran *Boatfile* (above). But his wife Dame Naomi James had the twin consolations of breaking the woman's record handsomely and being the only woman skipper to complete the course this time. Her time in *Kriter lady* was under 26 days.

Phil Weld's race winner *Moxie* was built specially for the 1980 race because his other trimaran was too big.

Seas had opened a split in the main hull and Loizeau was forced to retire and limp home.

A similar problem had beset Birch's *Olympus Photo*. There was a crash and a three-foot-square area of the underside of his trimaran's bridge deck ripped away. Birch said afterwards that he would like to think it was caused by some piece of wreckage in the water, but he believes it was simply through continuously crashing into waves at speed. Whatever the cause, it made Birch slow the boat and take time to effect makeshift repairs. He decided to push on to Newport, but let the race committee know that he now considered himself out of the running. But being Mike Birch, sailing conservatively meant still covering many miles each day and he never dropped far behind the leaders.

Less fortunate in that first week were Jacques Timsit and Nicholas Clifton. Both lost their yachts and had to be rescued. The Frenchman's *Motorola* — the renamed *Arauna IV* which had finished ninth in 1976 — was only two days out when she struck some wreckage while the skipper was asleep and started taking water so fast that she was obviously going to sink. Timsit took to his life raft and was plucked from the sea by an RAF helicopter 190 miles from Land's End. Clifton, too, was picked up from his life raft.

But Tom Grossman's big trimaran was going like a train. leaving Plymouth 26½ hours behind the rest after those hasty repairs, the dynamic American urged his boat across the sea faster than any other yacht in the fleet. He averaged 236 miles a day for the first week and was soon overhauling the tail-enders.

Then came the first breakdowns in the Argos location system. It had functioned perfectly in the French double-handed race in 1979, but then the antennae were put on the decks of each boat, with the electronic gear and batteries below in the dry. This time, to make it possible for a skipper to take the whole thing into the life raft if necessary, the complete unit was on deck, encased in a reputedly impermeable plastic casing. It transpired later that the casings were not up to standard. Some became brittle and cracked, letting in moisture to deplete the batteries. When there were no 'sightings' of Bertie Reed's *Voortrekker* and Philip Steggall's *Jeans Foster* on the first Thursday of the race, the authorities were alerted. But both yachts were soon traced by other means and it became clear that it was only their transponders which were at fault. Eventually nearly one third of the

Above. The Weld family turned out in strength aboard *Rogue Wave* to welcome the triumphant *Moxie* as she crossed the line. Phil's wife Anne (in dark glasses) scans the horizon expectantly. Below. *Moxie* creams through a froth of welcoming boats to cross the finish line bathed in early morning sunshine.

Weld's victory in *Moxie* was the result of superb organisation and absolute commitment. Only as *Moxie* sped sparklingly to the finish did the American veteran stop the constant search for his relentless pursuers.

fleet went 'silent', but fortunately they all had other rescue beacons available if necessary and the main inconvenience was the lack of a clear picture of which boats held which positions. We were back to the old practice of saying 'This boat seems to be leading from that one, but we haven't spotted so-and-so and there's always the chance that thingummy might have overtaken them during that spell of northerlies'. Some of the traditionalists thought that was as it should be.

But one Argos transmitter kept 'bleeping' faithfully — that on Phil Weld's 51-foot *Moxie*. As the second week of the race passed it became clear that the 65-year-old retired newspaper publisher was pulling well clear of the rest and heading inexorably for the first American win in the history of the race. The turning point seemed to have come about eight days out. Then a sharp depression had swept across the fleet, with stronger winds, as usual, towards its northern boundaries. The French front runners, especially Riguidel's *VSD*, and the early pace-setter *Paul Ricard*, were up there, going for the shortest route to Newport. Weld had studied the weather charts for the North Atlantic for June over the past 30 years and decided a more southerly course was not only safer but faster. 'The French must like it cold,' he radioed to the Observer office.

He proved his point that second week. While the other front runners slowed in the heavier going he galloped on across the ocean to be south of the eastern tip of Nova Scotia by the next weekend and clear of all challengers. *Paul Ricard's* roller furling headstay was giving Pajot problems and he was reported to be going to Newfoundland for help; *VSD* had shed a huge section of her cross-arm fairing and Riguidel was easing off for fear of more serious structural damage; Jean-Yves Terlain had turned the big catamaran *Gautier I* back with electrical problems; Michel Horeau found a break in the cross-arm of his big trimaran and also turned away to France; only Olivier de Kersauson in the monohull *Kriter VI* and Alain Labbe with *Hydrofolie* were within 500 miles of the leader. With the tally of failed Argos transponders now up to 30, it was not the happiest scene for the French.

So the challenge to Weld's supremacy over the last lap, if there was to be one, would have to come from an English-speaking yachtsman. Walter Greene was by now going famously and just ahead of Nick Keig. Birch was close up too, damaged boat or not, while Steggall had become the dark horse, unsighted by the satellites but known to be near enough to finish in

Under the Argos system, every yacht competing in the 1980 Observer Singlehanded sent constant messages up to circling satellites from automatic transponder units. The satellites re-transmitted the position data to ground telemetry stations — one in France, two in the United States. The information was then sent to Washington, passed on to Toulouse for processing and then distributed to the race information centres.

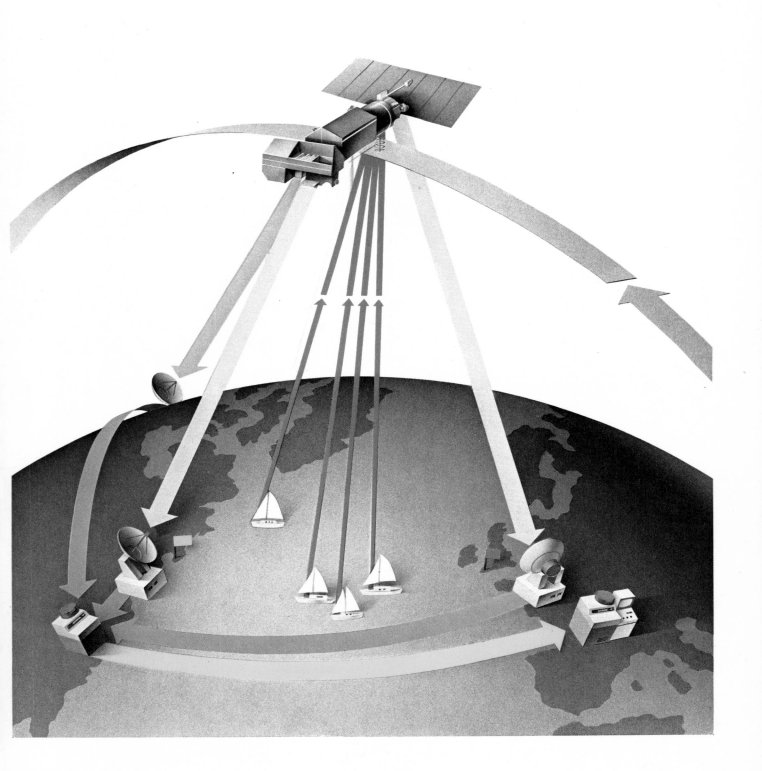

The joy of fulfilment is plain to see on the face of Phil Weld as he takes *Moxie* over the finish line at Brenton Reef, just outside Newport.

the frame. Jaworski was not being tracked either, but the early form of *Spaniel II* made her favourite to be first monohull to Newport, with an outside chance of snatching the honours if the weather turned nasty.

It did just the opposite. For the leaders, the run down from Cape Sable to Nantucket and the finish turned out to be a frustrating fumble through fogs and calms. The early estimates that Weld might reach the line 16 days after the start had to be extended to 17 and then perhaps 18.

But as dusk fell on Tuesday 24 June, those of us waiting for the winners in Newport planned an all-night vigil. The Weld family and Dick Newick were going out in the small hours in *Rogue Wave* to welcome the triumphant smaller sister; the television crews and press photographers were hoping that the swift *Moxie* would not appear until dawn had broken. And so it turned out. As yet another scorching June day blossomed in Rhode Island, the gleaming white hulls of *Moxie* came skimming over the waters of Newport Sound into the sharp morning sunlight. A huge fleet of motor cruisers and yachts filled with exultant Americans churned the waters of Brenton Reef into a maelstrom and the cacophony of their horns as *Moxie* passed the Brenton Tower must have wakened any lie-abed for miles around.

For Weld himself, it was a crowning moment. After those frustrating third places in two Round Britain Races and the Route du Rhum; after the despair of finding *Rogue Wave* was too big for the 1980 race; after the calculated gamble of building a new trimaran just for this one chance of glory, it was a marvellous reward to come flashing into the cheering effulgence of that triumphant morning. And as we worked out that *Moxie* had come from Plymouth in 48 minutes under the 18-day span and taken an incredible two days and 14 hours off Colas's record which had stood for eight years, we also realised that Weld had scored another bull's-eye. The best part of a year before this race he had written an article for the American *Sail* magazine, predicting the outcome — a win in 425 hours. 'On Wednesday 25 June, 1980, a trimaran whose skipper has managed to achieve all that has been suggested — high standards of mental and physical fitness, flawless self-steering, weather knowledge and good navigation technique — will win the Observer Singlehanded Transatlantic Race', he wrote. 'But he'd best not get a swelled head, because he'll be followed within 24 hours by six other boats, any one of whom might have won had they had his luck.'

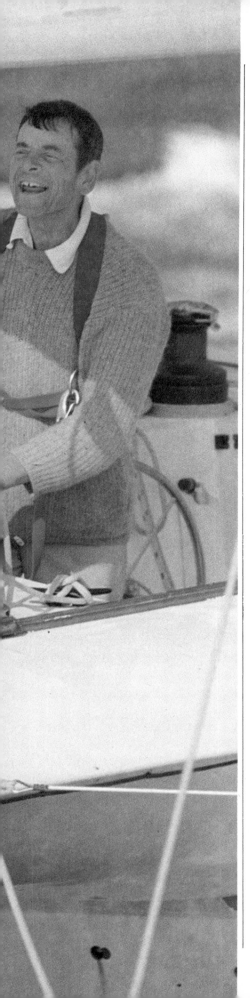

It was a prophecy which came true almost to the letter. *Moxie* — a trimaran — did finish that day, only six hours slower than that 425-hour target. And she was followed in within 24 hours by five, not six other boats, which could well have won. Second in was a delighted Nick Keig, almost exactly seven hours behind, with the dark horse Steggall only 40 minutes behind him. Then Mike Birch came in half an hour behind Steggall, delightedly holding aloft the great chunk of his yacht which had been crashed away by the waves.

Pajot, disappointed and dispirited, brought the menacing grey hulk of *Paul Ricard* to the line 6½ hours behind Birch while Walter Greene crossed with *Chausettes Olympia* 18 hours behind the leader to take fifth place in the official list. It was like one of those motor racing Grands Prix where a gaggle of cars comes down the final straight in close company and flashes past the chequered flag within a few seconds. In the class lists, Weld, Keig and Birch took the first three places in the Pen Duick category, and Steggall and Greene were first and second in Gipsy Moth. The third place went to the first Frenchman home — Daniel Gilard in *Brittany Ferries*, which finished in eighth place overall, behind the first two monohulls, Jaworski's *Spaniel II* and Austoni's *Chica Boba II*.

The first Jester class finisher did not arrive until nine days after *Moxie*. It was Jerry Cartwright in the fast little Beneteau boat *Le First*. He made it an American triumph by becoming the third class winner from the United States and crossing the line on the fourth of July. It was astonishing to realise that his time of one hour under 27 days would have been fast enough to beat Tabarly in 1964 and to take third place in 1968 — in a yacht which measured less than 30 feet overall; so much have the standards of the Observer Singlehanded been forced up over the years. Second in the Jester class was the English skipper John Chaundy, with his Rival 32 called — for the race anyway — *Free Newspapers*. Ian Radford, a veteran of the 1972 race, took third in Jester by lopping six days off his previous time with *Jubulisieve* to finish in 30½ days.

Dame Naomi James lost the domestic duel with Rob. He was 16th home in just under 23 days, while she finished 24th, three days later. But her time of 25 days 19 hours and 12 minutes was well inside the old Clare Francis record of just over 29 days.

The saddest story of the 1980 race was probably that of Czeslaw Gogolkiewicz, from Poland. Having sailed the 56-foot *Raczynski II* to

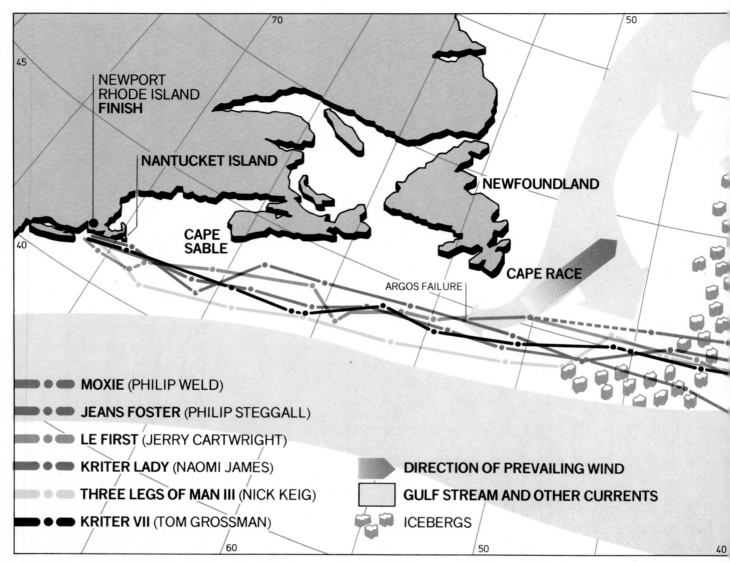

MOXIE (PHILIP WELD)

JEANS FOSTER (PHILIP STEGGALL)

LE FIRST (JERRY CARTWRIGHT)

KRITER LADY (NAOMI JAMES)

THREE LEGS OF MAN III (NICK KEIG)

KRITER VII (TOM GROSSMAN)

DIRECTION OF PREVAILING WIND

GULF STREAM AND OTHER CURRENTS

ICEBERGS

NEWPORT
RHODE ISLAND
FINISH

NANTUCKET ISLAND

NEWFOUNDLAND

CAPE SABLE

CAPE RACE

ARGOS FAILURE

Routes of the trophy-takers. Phil Weld's success in *Moxie* was closely keyed to his clever choice of track – just enough south of the Great Circle route to avoid the worst conditions of the depressions crossing the Atlantic, but not so far down that he lost time covering unnecessary distance or risked the adverse effects of the westward-flowing Gulf Stream. Jerry Cartwright's high average speed in *Le First* – which earned him the Jester trophy – was also due to good tactics and constant determined sailing. Tom Grossman's *Kriter VII* was actually travelling faster than any other yacht in the fleet after her delayed start 26½ hours behind the

within a few miles of the finish line, he had the bad luck to collide with a fishing boat during one of the many murky nights of that early July. The trawl arm of the fisherman crashed across his deck, sweeping away mast, rig, sails and very nearly the skipper too. The yacht had to be towed to Point Judith at the mouth of Narragansett Bay by the American Coastguard.

But in the final analysis the retirement rate for the race was modest — 17 yachts pulled out for one reason or another, and just two failed to make Newport before the 50-day time limit ran out — they were the old faithful, *Jester*, which had been back to Plymouth for repairs and then put into the Azores for more attention, and *Old Navy Lights*, the yacht entered by the first Greek in the race's history. Antonios Vassiliades finally made it to America three days after the deadline.

But 72 of the original 91 starters completed the course in under 50 days, and every one of them had gripping stories to tell of the crossing. There was Tom Grossman, for example, explaining how he had powered through to tenth place, despite that delayed start and a time penalty for being late for scrutineering in Plymouth. There was the quiet American

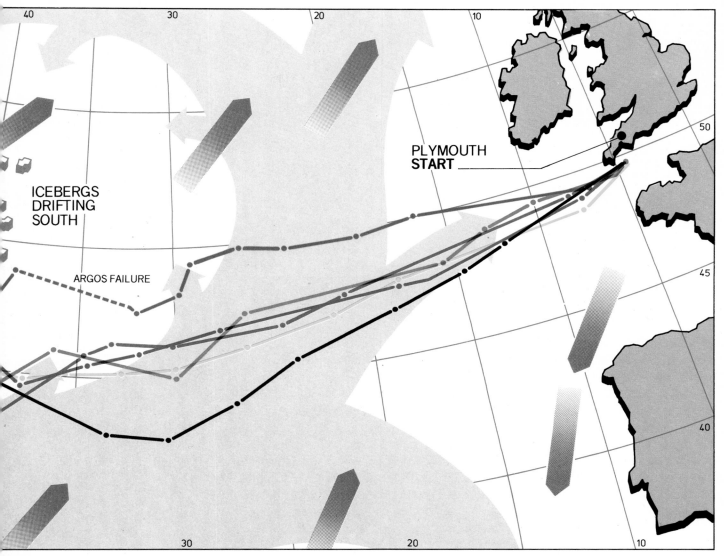

ICEBERGS
DRIFTING
SOUTH

ARGOS FAILURE

PLYMOUTH
START

Bill Doelger, modestly recounting how he had managed to re-rig his Val trimaran *Edith* after the mast had come down in mid-Atlantic — a stupefying piece of brave seamanship. There was the Dutchman Kees Roemers, showing his illustrated log, with one vivid drawing of a close encounter with a fishing boat only feet away in the fog and a boy's astonished voice over the water — 'It's a sailing yacht!' And there was the Belgian Oscar Debra, arriving in Newport at last after 12 years of trying.

It had been the fastest, the best-reported and — I believe — the happiest race in the Observer Singlehanded series, with an international camaraderie running through the fleet — and through the results, too. There were eleven different nations represented in the first 20 yachts home. That can only be beneficial to the event's future. But it seems to me particularly pleasing that the United States should have done so well this time in the race which finishes in her own water. And I don't think there was a single skipper in the fleet who would begrudge the dazzling victory to that most popular of Americans, Phil Weld. The oldest man in the race, the most-liked and, quite simply the best singlehander of them all.

others, but he could not maintain the differential long enough to overhaul the front runners Weld, Keig and Steggall. Dame Naomi James's constant good daily mileages added up to a new record for the solo trip across the Atlantic by a woman sailor – beating the time set by Clare Francis in the 1976 Observer Singlehanded.

CHAPTER 8

TRICK'S END

THE OBSERVER SINGLEHANDED has changed hugely during its 20-year lifetime. From friendly tussle disputed by a tiny band of apparently quite nutty pioneers trying to do the impossible, the competition has grown into one of the best-known international sailing events in the calendar. It has helped to make famous the names of seminal influences in the world of yachting, such as Francis Chichester, Eric Tabarly, Derek Kelsall, Alain Colas, Dick Newick, Jean—Yves Terlain, Walter Greene, Clare Francis and Phil Weld, to name but a few. It has also speeded the development of many pieces of yacht equipment which now ease the lot of any short-handed sailor — reliable self-steering gear, self-tailing winches, furling headsails and roll-up mains, solar panels and wind generators, lugsail rigs, easy-cook meals and radar detectors. Again the list could be extended. It has prompted the design and construction of some of the most innovative sailing craft to take to the water during the second half of the twentieth century — the original *Pen Duick II;* the revolutionary proa *Cheers;* the slim three-master *Vendredi 13,* the massive schooner *Club Méditerranée;* the powerful catamaran *British Oxygen (Kriter III);* the extraordinary hydrofoil sailing machine *Paul Ricard,* and the whole fleet of light, fast and exciting trimarans which have flown from the board of Dick Newick — *Three Cheers, The Third Turtle, Kriter VII, Olympus Photo* and, of course, *Moxie.*

With the 1980 Race, the Singlehanded took yet another decisive step forward. By limiting the size of the craft competing and the numbers in the fleet and then equipping each yacht with satellite tracking transponders, the organisers set new standards of safety and responsibility for what some critics see as a foolhardy and dangerous event.

There *is* an element of danger in sailing singlehanded across the Atlantic. Yet is is worth noting that in the six races to date, no less than 326 yachts have set out to sail to America and 223 have succeeded. Of the 100 or so not completing the passage, the majority have retired because of some gear damage, without involving any rescue assistance, while some others have reached the finish but outside the time limit. Only two skippers have been lost. What is more, no competing boat has ever caused injury to anyone not in the race. With the restricted fleet and the Argos equipment to keep it under constant surveillance, the 1980 race became not only better-

Start of the 1980 race, with Walter Greene's *Chaussettes Olympia* (35) slicing through the churning waters of Plymouth Sound to an early class lead.

Two yachts built specially to win the Observer Singlehanded. Tabarly's 1964 *Pen Duick II,* left, was just 44 feet long, built on a shoe-string budget. But she won. Colas's 1976 *Club Méditerránee,* right, was 236 feet long, cost hundreds of thousands, and finished second.

Three Cheers has been one of the seminal influences in the Observer race. She started among the favourites in both 1972 and 1976 and her near-sister ship **Olympus Photo** was fourth in 1980 despite speed-sapping damage.

publicised but also decidedly safer.

The future must be bright. The next Observer Singlehanded is planned for 1984, to be organised, as ever, by the Royal Western Yacht Club in Plymouth and once more sponsored by The Observer. It is unlikely that there will be any major changes when the rules and conditions are published towards the end of 1980; the great success of the sixth race in the series, despite the limits so many distrusted, must encourage the race committee to stand by the proven formula. But one major change will disrupt the settled pattern of the last 20 years. Colonel Jack Odling-Smee will no longer be chairman of the committee. Now 72, he is giving up the job he has done so well during the whole span of the event.

Before the 1984 Observer Singlehanded there is to be another race across the Atlantic which could well become a classic: a double-handed race on the same course, to be sailed in 1981. It will have the same organisers and promoters, with the Europe 1 radio station again joining the sponsorship support to underwrite the cost of the Argos transponders which will be fixed to each yacht. Already the provisional entry list bristles with exciting names: Tabarly, Birch, Blyth, Greene, Fehlmann, Knox-Johnston, Malinovsky, Terlain, Vidal, Weld, Gliksman, Keig, Pajot, Luhrs, James, Grossman and Riguidel.

The double-handed race seems certain of success already, but whatever acclaim it earns there is little chance that it will ever displace the Singlehanded in the hearts and minds of the millions arounds the world who follow these heroic competitions. The Observer race, or La Transat, as the French call it, has become the longest-established, most famous, best-organised and most prestigious of all the short-handed sailing races. Like Wimbledon, the Epsom Derby or the Cup Final, it has an aura all its own. And like those classic events, to win it means more than to take any other glittering prize. Phil Weld called his all-conquering trimaran *Moxie* after a tonic drink which was once very popular in the New England area of the United States. As a joke, he had T-shirts and leaflets printed with the promotional message of the Moxie makers of 1876. 'It gives a durable solid strength, makes you eat voraciously and takes away the tired, sleepy, lifeless feeling like magic.' Weld's famous victory in the 1980 race certainly did all of that for him. And there is no doubt that this great race will go on providing just such a tonic for every future sailor who succeeds in the great challenge – to sail alone against the Atlantic.

THE OBSERVER SINGLEHANDED TRANSATLANTIC RACE
RESULTS

1960

PLACE	SKIPPER	NATION	YACHT	TIME TAKEN
1	**Francis Chichester**	Britain	*Gipsy Moth III*	40 days
2	**Blondie Hasler**	Britain	*Jester*	48 days
3	**David Lewis**	Britain	*Cardinal Vertue*	56 days
4	**Val Howells**	Britain	*Eira*	63 days
5	**Jean Lacombe**	France	*Cap Horn*	74 days

1964

PLACE	SKIPPER	NATION	YACHT	TIME TAKEN
1	**Eric Tabarly**	France	*.Pen Duick II*	27 03 56
2	**Francis Chichester**	Britain	*Gipsy Moth III*	29 23 57
3	**Val Howells**	Britain	*Akka*	32 18 08
4	**Alec Rose**	Britain	*Lively Lady*	36 17 30
5	**Blondie Hasler**	Britain	*Jester*	37 22 05
6	**Bill Howell**	Australia	*Stardrift*	38 03 23
7	**David Lewis**	Britain	*Rehu Moana*	38 12 04
8	**Mike Ellison**	Britain	*Ilala*	46 06 26
9	**Jean Lacombe**	France	*Golif*	46 07 05
10	**Bob Bunker**	Britain	*Vanda Caelea*	49 18 45
11	**Mike Butterfield**	Britain	*Misty Miller*	53 00 05
12	**Geoffrey Chaffey**	Britain	*Ericht 2*	60 11 15
13	**Derek Kelsall**	Britain	*Folatre*	61 14 04
14	**Axel Pederson**	Denmark	*Marco Polo*	63 13 30

Tammie Norie (Robin McCurdy) retired.

1968

PLACE	SKIPPER	NATION	YACHT	TIME TAKEN		
1	**Geoffey Williams**	Britain	*Sir Thomas Lipton*	25	20	33
2	**Bruce Dalling**	South Africa	*Voortrekker*	26	13	42
3	**Tom Follett**	U.S.A.	*Cheers*	27	00	13
4	**Leslie Williams**	Britain	*Spirit of Cutty Sark*	29	10	17
5	**Bill Howell**	Australia	*Golden Cockerel*	31	16	24
6	**Brian Cooke**	Britain	*Opus*	34	08	23
7	**Martin Minter-Kemp**	Britain	*Gancia Girl*	34	13	15
8	**Noel Bevan**	Britain	*Myth of Malham*	36	01	41
9	**Bernard de Castelbajac**	France	*Maxine*	37	13	47
10	**Jean-Yves Terlain**	France	*Maguelonne*	38	09	10
11	**Nigel Burgess**	Britain	*Dogwatch*	38	12	13
12	**André Foezon**	France	*Silvia II*	40	00	16
13	**Bertil Enbom**	Sweden	*Fione*	40	14	13
14	**Claus Hehner**	Germany	*Mex*	41	10	46
15	**Stephen Pakenham**	Britain	*Rob Roy*	42	03	49
16	**Colin Forbes**	Britain	*Starlted Faun*	45	10	08
17	**Bernard Rodriguez**	U.S.A.	*Amistad*	47	18	05
18	**Ake Mattson**	Sweden	*Goodwin II*	50	19	48
19	**Michael Richey**	Britain	*Jester*	57	10	40

Goodwin II finished 18th but was not officially classified since she was disqualified for taking on stores during the race.

Retirements:
Pen Duick IV (Eric Tabarly) Collision and steering trouble.
Coila (Eric Williams) Skipper's illness.
San Giorgio (Alec Corozzo) Rudder problems.
Atlantis III (David Pyle) Steering failure.
Wileca (William Wallin) Too cold.
Tamoure (Bernard Waquet) Unable to navigate.
Koala III (Edith Baumann) Sank.
Zeevalk (Robert Wingate) Leak in hull.

White Ghost (Michael Pulsford) Steering failure.
Aye-Aye (Egon Heinemann) Steering failure.
Gunther III (Guy Piazzini) Mast loose.
Ocean Highlander (Sandy Munro) Dismasted.
La Delirante (Lionel Paillard) Dismasted.
Raph (Alain Gliksman) Broken rudder.
Abrima (Marc Cuiklinski) Sank.

1972

PLACE	SKIPPER	NATION	YACHT	TIME TAKEN
1	**Alain Colas**	France	*Pen Duick IV*	20 13 15
2	**Jean-Yves Terlain**	France	*Vendredi 13*	21 05 14
3	**Jean-Marie Vidal**	France	*Cap 33*	24 05 40
4	**Brian Cooke**	Britain	*British Steel*	24 19 28
5	**Tom Follett**	U.S.A.	*Three Cheers*	27 11 04
6	**Gerard Pestey**	France	*Architeuthis*	28 11 55
7	**Martin Minter-Kemp**	Britain	*Strongbow*	28 12 46
8	**Alain Gliksman**	France	*Toucan*	28 12 54
9	**Franco Faggioni**	Italy	*Sagittario*	28 23 05
10	**Jim Ferris**	U.S.A.	*Whisper*	29 11 15
11	**Marc Linski**	France	*Isles du Frioul*	30 02 45
12	**Chris Baranowski**	Poland	*Polonez*	30 16 55
13	**Mike McMullen**	Britain	*Binkie II*	31 18 10
14	**Marie-Claude Fauroux**	France	*Aloa VII*	32 22 51
15	**Jock Brazier**	Britain	*Flying Angel*	33 09 21
16	**Joel Charpentier**	France	*Wild Rocket*	34 13 38
17	**Yves Olivaux**	France	*Aloa I*	34 17 30
18	**Guy Piazzini**	Switzerland	*Cambronne*	35 10 24
19	**Pierre Chassin**	France	*Concorde*	36 01 19
20	**Bruce Webb**	Britain	*Gazelle*	36 02 07
21	**John Holtom**	Britain	*La Bamba of Mersea*	36 04 30
22	**Guy Hornett**	Britain	*Blue Smoke*	36 21 26
23	**Wolf Kirchner**	Germany	*White Dolphin*	38 07 17
24	**Jock McLeod**	Britain	*Ron Glas*	38 09 50
25	**Richard Clifford**	Britain	*Shamaal*	38 10 30
26	**Bob Lancy Burn**	U.S.A.	*Blue Gipsy*	39 08 30
27	**Phil Weld**	U.S.A.	*Trumpeter*	39 13 25
28	**Claus Hehner**	Germany	*Mex*	40 08 23
29	**Ambrogio Fogar**	Italy	*Surprise*	41 04 45
30	**Pat Chilton**	Britain	*Mary Kate of Arun*	41 17 17
31	**Eric Sumner**	Britain	*Francette*	43 09 38
32	**Zbigniew Pulchalski**	Poland	*Miranda*	45 10 05
33	**Heiko Krieger**	Germany	*Tinie*	46 15 30
34	**Jerry Cartwright**	U.S.A.	*Scuffler III*	49 02 00
35	**Chris Elliott**	Britain	*Lauric*	51 14 33
36	**Andrew Spedding**	Britain	*Summersong*	51 23 05
37	**David Blagden**	Britain	*Willing Griffin*	52 11 06
38	**Teresa Remiszewska**	Poland	*Komodor*	57 03 18
39	**Michael Richey**	Britain	*Jester*	58 08 18
40	**Anne Michailof**	France	*P.S.*	59 06 12

Nike (Richard Konkolski), *Casper* (Martin Wills) and *Golden Vanity* (Peter Crowther) all reached Newport after the 60 day time limit had expired.

Retirements:
Olva II (Oscar Debra) Split fuel tank.
Gipsy Moth V (Sir Francis Chichester) Damaged by French weather ship.
Tahiti Bill (Bill Howell) Collision with trawler.
Second Life (Gerard Dijkstra) Dismasted
Mersea Pearl (Bob Miller) Dismasted

Lady of Fleet (Murray Sayle) Dismasted
Tuloa (Harry Mitchell) Leak in hull.
Onyx (Eugene Riguidel) Rigging failure.
Namar IV (Edoardo Guzzetti) Illness of skipper.
Justa Listang (Bob Salmon) Dismasted
Bristol Fashion (Max Barton) Dismasted
Chica Boba (Carlo Mascheroni) Illness of skipper.

1976

PLACE	SKIPPPER	NATION	YACHT	TIME TAKEN
1	**Eric Tabarly**	France	*Pen Duick VI*	23 20 12
2	**Alain Colas**	France	*Club Méditerannée*	24 03 36
3	**Mike Birch**	Canada	*The Third Turtle*	24 20 39
4	**Kazimierz Jaworski**	Poland	*Spaniel*	24 23 40
5	**Tom Grossman**	U.S.A.	*Cap 33*	26 08 15
6	**Jean-Claude Parisis**	France	*Petrouchka*	27 00 55
7	**David Palmer**	Britain	*FT*	27 07 46
8	**Walter Greene**	U.S.A.	*Friends*	27 10 37
9	**Jacques Timsit**	France	*Arauna IV*	27 15 32
10	**Alain Gabbay**	France	*Objectif Sud 3*	28 09 58
11	**Francis Stokes**	U.S.A.	*Moonshine*	28 12 46
12	**Carlo Bianchi**	Italy	*Venilia*	29 00 15
13	**Clare Francis**	Britain	*Robertson's Golly*	29 01 52
14	**Gustaaf Versluys**	Belgium	*Tyfoon V*	29 21 12
15	**John de Trafford**	Britain	*Quest*	30 07 39
16	**Yves Anrys**	Belgium	*Pawn of Nieuwpoort*	30 15 34
17	**Eugene Riguidel**	France	*Nova*	30 15 34
18	**Gilles Vaton**	France	*Ackel France*	31 03 12
19	**Daniel Pierre**	France	*Lorca*	31 14 45
20	**Patrice Dumas**	France	*Sirtec*	31 23 09
21	**Guy Hornett**	Britain	*Old Moore's Almanack*	32 02 06
22	**Bill Howell**	Australia	*Tahiti Bill*	32 05 19
23	**Geoffrey Hales**	Britain	*Wild Rival*	32 13 48
24	**Bernard Pallard**	France	*Petit Breton*	32 19 57
25	**Folkmar Graf**	Germany	*Dadztoy II*	32 20 55
26	**Ernesto Raab**	Italy	*Carina*	33 01 22
27	**Rome Ryott**	Britain	*Adhara*	33 02 54
28	**Guy Riboulet**	France	*Pierre*	33 03 39
29	**Gerd Buckling**	Germany	*Helene III*	33 08 41
30	**Richard Clifford**	Britain	*Shamaal II*	33 12 51
31	**E. Everett Smith**	U.S.A.	*Wind Quest*	34 08 44
32	**Burg Veenemans**	Belgium	*Pytheas*	34 10 10
33	**Nicholas Clifton**	Britain	*Azulao*	35 03 35
34	**John Mansell**	New Zealand	*Innovator of Mana*	35 12 25
35	**Philip Howells**	Britain	*Fromstock Filius*	35 16 07
36	**Don Clark**	Britain	*Freemerle*	35 22 50
37	**Georgi Georgiev**	Bulgaria	*Kor Karoli*	36 01 50
38	**Yves Olivaux**	France	*Patriarche*	36 05 14
39	**Ian Radford**	Britain	*Jabulisiwe*	36 08 44
40	**Lars Walgren**	Sweden	*Swedlady*	36 11 10
41	**Edoardo Austoni**	Italy	*Chica Boba*	37 06 00
42	**Ida Castiglioni**	Italy	*Eva*	37 08 20
43	**Elie Labourgade**	France	*Avaloa*	37 10 24
44	**Klaus Schrodt**	Germany	*Lilliam*	37 21 25
45	**Jock McLeod**	Britain	*Ron Glas*	38 17 40
46	**Rory Nugent**	U.S.A.	*Edith*	39 04 30
47	**Chris Butler**	Britain	*Achilles Neuf*	39 06 02

PLACE	SKIPPPER	NATION	YACHT	TIME TAKEN		
48	**Juan Guiu**	Spain	*Crisan*	39	08	15
49	**Richard Konkolski**	Czechoslovakia	*Nike*	39	10	49
50	**James Young**	Britain	*English Rose IV*	39	11	29
51	**Peter Crowther**	Britain	*Galway Blazer*	39	12	57
52	**David White**	U.S.A.	*Catapha*	39	17	15
53	**Harry Mitchell**	Britain	*Tuloa*	41	11	59
54	**Ennque Vidal Paz**	Spain	*Castanuela*	42	10	10
55	**David Pyle**	Britain	*Westward*	42	10	11
56	**Zbigniev Puchalski**	Poland	*Miranda*	42	13	14
57	**Wolfgang Wanders**	Germany	*Amitie*	42	17	30
58	**Henk Jukkema**	Holland	*Hesperia*	42	21	18
59	**Max Bourgeois**	France	*Achille*	43	08	41
60	**Corrado di Majo**	Italy	*Tikka III*	44	00	37
61	**David Sutcliffe**	Britain	*Lady Anne of St Donats*	44	03	47
62	**Angelo Preden**	Italy	*Caipirinha*	44	04	45
63	**Stuart Woods**	Ireland	*Golden Harp*	44	19	14
64	**Martin Wills**	Britain	*Casper*	44	21	15
65	**Richard Elliott**	Britain	*Lauric*	45	02	29
66	**Henry Pottle**	Britain	*Janina*	45	03	12
67	**Michel Bourgeois**	France	*Dragon*	45	12	45
68	**David Cowper**	Britain	*Airedale*	46	11	17
69	**Nigel Lang**	Britain	*Galadriel of Lotharien*	48	03	10
70	**Rodney Kendall**	New Zealand	*Songeur*	49	05	40
71	**Gerard Dijkstra**	Holland	*Bestevaer*	49	07	22
72	**Eilco Kasemier**	Holland	*Bylgia*	49	10	34
73	**Robert Lengyel**	U.S.A.	*Prodigal*	49	19	30

Retirements:

Kervilor (Guy Cornou) Skipper injured.
Aquarius (André de Jong) Broken steering.
Bollemaat (Kees Roemers) Battery problems.
McArthur (Hywel Price) Faulty rudder.
Objectif Sud I (Marc Linski) Broken steering.
Namar 5 (Edoardo Guzzetti) Broken steering.
Arctic Skua (Mike Richardson) Broken steering.
Toria (Tony Bullimore) Caught fire and sank.
Flying Angel (Jock Brazier) Damaged steering.
Karate (Pierre-Yves Charbonnier) Skipper injured.
5100 (Dominique Berthier) Sank after collision.
Wild Rocket (Joel Charpentier) Rig failure.
Ek Soeki (John Christian) Skipper ill.
Kriter III (Jean-Yves Terlain) Broke up and sank.
Jester (Mike Richey) Retired, no damage.
Unibrass Brython (Val Howells) Skipper injured.
Gauloises (Pierre Fehlmann) Sprang leak and sank.
Keep Cap D'Adge (Jean-Claud Montesinos) Retired.
Pronuptia (C.H. Le Moing) Sail problems.
Tumult (Chris Smith) Skipper ill.
ITT Oceanic (Yvon Fauconnier) Skipper injured.
Altergo (C.S.W. Ward) Gear breakage.
Panda 31 (Paolo Mascheroni) Retired.
Ironiguy (Guy Brunet) Broken steering.
Croda Way (Mike Best) Structural damage.
Nyarlathotep (P. Szekely) Sank.

Vanessa (Oscar Debra) Retired.
Silke (Hans Schulte) Boat leaking.
CS e RB II Busnelli (Doi Malingri) Collision damage.
Aceteia II (Christian Le Mercer) Collision damage.
Spirit of America (Mike Kane) Stuctural damage.
Gillygaloo (Andrew Bray) Damaged steering.
Sleuth Hound (Colin Drummond) Mast damage.
Drakar III (Alain Marcel) Damaged steering.
Jade (R.J. Ogle) Electrical failure.
Tinie II (Heiko Krieger) Mast damage.
Pen-Ar-Bed (Gerard Frigout) Broken steering.
Spirit of Surprise (Ambrogio Fogar) Structural damage.
Galloping Gael (Mike Flanagan) Skipper disappeared.
Demon Demo (Angus Primrose) Capsized and dismasted.
Valitalia (Paolo Sciarretta) Retired.
Logo (Aline Marchand) Dismasted.
Silmaril (Patrick O'Donovan) Dismasted.
Sharavoge (Jonathan Virden) Retired for lack of wind.
Kylie (Simon Hunter) Retired for lack of wind.
Three Cheers (Mike McMullen) Yacht and skipper disappeared.
Five yachts reached Newport after the 50-day time limit expired. They were: *True North* (Brian Start – Canada); *Bluff* (Rod White – Britain); *Meinwen* (Peter Evans – Britain); *Bigoudon Brise* (Jean Ropert – France); and *Bally Claire* (Dr F. Sloan – Britain).

1980

PLACE	SKIPPER	NATION	YACHT	TIME TAKEN
1	**Phil Weld**	U.S.A.	*Moxie*	17 23 12
2	**Nick Keig**	Britain	*Three Legs of Mann III*	18 06 04
3	**Philip Steggall**	U.S.A.	*Jeans Foster*	18 06 45
4	**Mike Birch**	Canada	*Olympus Photo*	18 07 15
5	**Walter Green**	U.S.A.	*Chaussettes Olympia*	18 17 29
6	**Kazimierz Jaworski**	Poland	*Spaniel II*	19 13 25
7	**Edoardo Austoni**	Italy	*Chica Boba II*	20 02 30
8	**Daniel Gilard**	France	*Brittany Ferries*	21 00 09*
9	**Richard Konkolski**	Czechoslovakia	*Nike II*	21 06 21
10	**Tom Grossman**	U.S.A.	*Kriter VII*	21 08 01*
11	**Wolfgang Wanders**	Germany	*Stadt Krefeld*	21 14 22
12	**Gustaaf Versluys**	Belgium	*Tyfoon VI*	21 15 01
13	**Alain Labbe**	France	*Hydrofolie*	21 16 41
14	**Olivier de Kersauson**	France	*Kriter VI*	21 20 30*
15	**Pierre Sicouri**	Italy	*Gui IV Fila*	22 02 34
16	**Rob James**	Britain	*Boatfile*	22 22 55
17	**Denis Gliksman**	France	*France Loisirs*	23 10 00
18	**Bertie Reed**	South Africa	*Voortrekker*	23 12 42
19	**Eugene Riguidel**	France	*VSD*	24 01 27*
20	**Philippe Fournier**	Switzerland	*Haute Nendaz*	24 03 05
21	**Jean-Pierre Millet**	France	*Open Space*	25 01 05
22	**Victor Sagi**	Spain	*Garuda*	25 08 23
23	**Francis Stokes**	U.S.A.	*Moonshine*	25 14 07
24	**Dame Naomi James**	New Zealand	*Kriter Lady*	25 19 12
25	**Bill Homewood**	U.S.A.	*The Third Turtle*	25 20 13
26	**Robert Bocinsky**	U.S.A.	*Ambergris*	26 00 39
27	**Jean-Jacques Jaouen**	France	*Les Menuires*	26 15 21
28	**Jerzy Rakowicz**	Poland	*Spaniel*	26 19 29
29	**Jerry Cartwright**	U.S.A.	*Le First*	26 22 55
30	**John Chaundy**	Britain	*Free Newspapers*	28 00 56
31	**Bill Doelger**	U.S.A.	*Edith*	28 04 10
32	**Uno Hylen**	Sweden	*Yoldia*	28 05 48
33	**Desmond Hampton**	Britain	*Wild Rival*	28 13 44
34	**John Charnley**	Britain	*Atlantic Harp*	29 06 21
35	**Ian Radford**	Britain	*Jubulisiwe*	30 14 38
36	**John Oswald**	Britain	*Basildon Moonshadow*	30 15 30
37	**Oscar Debra**	Belgium	*Crumpy Nut*	30 16 32
38	**Richard Clifford**	Britain	*Warrior Shamaal*	30 16 45
39	**Henk Jukkema**	Holland	*Victoria*	30 18 02
40	**Chris Smith**	Britain	*Sadler Bluejacket*	30 19 20
41	**Chris Butler**	Britain	*Achillea*	30 20 49
42	**Kees Roemers**	Holland	*Bollemaat IV*	30 21 24
43	**Angus Primrose**	Britain	*Demon of Hamble*	30 23 08
44	**Roger Forkert**	U.S.A.	*Parisien Liberé*	31 10 43
45	**Guy Bernardin**	France	*Ratso II*	31 11 45
46	**Jim Kyle**	U.S.A.	*Dream Weaver*	31 23 05
47	**Alain Veyron**	France	*Cat Marine*	32 02 50

PLACE	SKIPPPER	NATION	YACHT	TIME TAKEN
48	**Don Clark**	Britain	*Abacus*	32 07 17
49	**Thomas Gochberg**	U.S.A.	*Mistral*	32 18 35
50	**Luis Tonizzo**	U.S.A.	*Egret*	33 05 25
51	**Nikolai Djambazov**	Bulgaria	*Tangra*	34 10 53
52	**Wytze van der Zee**	Holland	*Black Pearl*	35 11 20
53	**Jose Ugarte**	Spain	*Northwind*	36 06 43
54	**Hank van de Weg**	Holland	*Tjisje*	36 22 22
55	**Paul Rodgers**	Britain	*Christian Saul II*	37 03 11
56	**Wolfgang Quix**	Germany	*Jeantex*	38 03 02
57	**Giampaolo Venturin**	Italy	*Cecco*	38 08 55
58	**Juan Guiu**	Spain	*Crisan*	38 13 43
59	**Jan Verwoerd**	Holland	*Seagull II*	38 17 00
60	**Bob Lush**	Canada	*Olympus Sailing*	39 01 46
61	**Tony Lush**	U.S.A.	*One Hand Clapping II*	39 06 56
62	**Andre de Jong**	Holland	*La Peligrosa*	39 16 55
63	**Bob Lengyel**	U.S.A.	*Prodigal*	40 06 09
64	**Tom Ryan**	U.S.A.	*Peggy*	40 20 16★
65	**Ernest Sonne**	U.S.A.	*Elbe*	41 10 45
66	**John Hunt**	U.S.A.	*Crystal Catfish III*	41 13 18
67	**John Beharrell**	Britain	*Miscin*	42 16 00
68	**Beppe Panada**	Italy	*Mu Lat*	42 18 20★
69	**Per Mustelin**	Finland	*Mare Atlantic*	42 23 34
70	**William Wallace**	U.S.A.	*Novia*	44 10 42
71	**Martin Wills**	Britain	*Casper*	46 13 52★
72	**Burg Veenemans**	Holland	*Pytheas II*	49 08 16★

★Includes time penalty

Old Navy Lights (Antonios Vassiliades, Greece) and *Jester* (Michael Richey, Britain) finished the course after the time limit expired.

Unofficial competitor

	Marc Pajot	France	*Paul Ricard*	18 13 41

Retirements

Miss Dubonnet (Florence Arthaud) Dismasted before start.
Jomada (Simon Hunter) Skipper's injury.
Silke (Hans Schulte) Forestay carried away.
Serta Perfectsleeper (Judith Lawson) Dismasted.
Motorola (Jacques Timsit) Sank.
Maurice Lidchi (Michel Horeau) Structural problems.
Tuesday's Child (Warren Luhrs) Keel problems.
Livery Dole (Peter Phillips) Sank after losing float.
Sea Quest (Mac Smith) Top halyard broken.

Raczynski II (Czeslaw Gogolkiewicz) Dismasted by trawler.
Roundabout (Theo Cockerell) Burnt out in Azores.
Lady Dona (Piet ter Laag) Skipper ill.
Brittany Ferries II (Bernard Pallard) Returned to France.
Mattia III (Antonio Chioatto) Sank.
Gauloises IV (Eric Loizeau) Holed in hull.
Fleury Michon (Nicholas Clifton) Capsized.
Charles Heidsieck (Jean-Claude Parisis) Broken rudder.
Gautier (Jean-Yves Terlain) Electrical problems.

INDEX

For Lukie, Georgie and Mionee

ACKNOWLEDGEMENTS:
DESIGN BY STANLEY GLAZER. COVER PHOTOGRAPH BY PAUL KENNEDY.
PHOTOGRAPHS BY:
MICK ALEXANDER, ALASTAIR BLACK, JANE BOWN, CHRIS BRASHER,
BRYN CAMPBELL, CHRIS CORMACK, JOHN HODDER, COLIN JARMAN,
PAUL KENNEDY, NEIL LIBBERT, EAMONN McCABE, TONY McGRATH,
DAVID NEWELL-SMITH, BOB SALMON, CHRIS SMITH.
MAPS BY THE DIAGRAM GROUP.

CREDITS TO:

CNES/ARGOS; CII HONEYWELL BULL; HONEYWELL UK/USA; BBC WORLD
SERVICE; RHODE ISLAND STATE YACHTING COMMITTEE; ROYAL
WESTERN YACHT CLUB; GOAT ISLAND YACHT CLUB; THE
METEOROLOGICAL OFFICE; EUROPE 1; GEOFF UNDERWOOD; GEOFF
HALES; MARTIN MINTER-KEMP.

TYPESETTING BY DACORUM GRAPHICS
REPRODUCTION AND PLATEMAKING BY BARRETT & BERKELEY
PRINTED BY IMPACT LITHO (TOLWORTH) LTD